Building the
SRI RAMA TEMPLE
in Ayodhya

BY THE SAME AUTHOR

Ayodhya Ram Temple and Hindu Renaissance

Economic Development and Reforms in India and China

Hindus Under Siege: The Way Out

Sri Lanka in Crisis: India's Options

Terrorism in India: A Strategy of Deterrence for India's National Security

Rama Setu: Symbol of National Unity

Corruption and Corporate Governance in India: Satyam, Spectrum and Sundaram

Hindutva and National Renaissance

India's China Strategic Perspective

Virat Hindu Identity: Concept and its Power

2G Spectrum Scam

The Ideology of India's Modern Right

Building the SRI RAMA TEMPLE in Ayodhya

Subramanian Swamy, Ph.D. (Harvard)

Member of Parliament, India
Former Union Cabinet Minister for Commerce, Law & Justice, India

HAR-ANAND
PUBLICATIONS PVT LTD

Reprint, 2026

Published by Ashok Gosain and Ashish Gosain for:
HAR-ANAND PUBLICATIONS PVT LTD
E-49/3, Okhla Industrial Area, Phase-II, New Delhi-110020
Tel: 41603491
E-mail: info@haranandbooks.com/haranand@rediffmail.com
Shop online at: www.haranandbooks.com

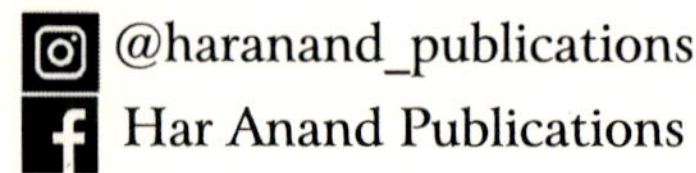
@haranand_publications
Har Anand Publications

Printed in India at Megha Enterprises

PREFACE

Religion has in modern India not been thought of as a force for shaping a moral society. Such negative thinking is considered as constituting "secularism." But this approach is erroneous. Sri Aurobindo said: "All great movements of life in India have begun with the new spiritual thought and usually a new religious activity." Even Jawaharlal Nehru ultimately at the fag end of his life acknowledged this truth in his foreword to one of Dr. Karan Singh book as follows: "It is significant to note that great political mass movements in India have had a spiritual background behind them."

A society based on dharma is vitally needed at this moment in our history, because there is a dimension to the current national crisis, namely, the moral decay and the decline of character in our society which if not stemmed, will slowly poison to death our nation.

This decay and decline is visible in every aspect of our life—politicians defecting for office and cash, bureaucrats taking bribes, teachers selling exam questions, students passing by cheating, businessmen adulterating products, lawyers cheating clients, doctors betraying their patients etc. To some extent such degeneration is there in every society, but the alarming aspect in India is the pace of this decay and the spread of it. Consequent to this decay is the wave of dangerous cynicism amongst the youth.

This moral decay has to be stemmed. A renaissance of values in society has to take place. How will this renaissance come about? And which leader shall be its instrument? For this, a leader shall be one who is committed to an ideology and determined to implement an agenda for renaissance.

In India, the majority is the conglomerate Hindu community which represents about 80% of the total Indian population, while minorities are constituted by Muslims [13%] and Christians [3%] Sikhs, Jains, Parsis, and some other small religious groups, with affinity to the Hindu's Sanatana Dharma represent the remaining four percent. But Sri Rama while revered by Hindus as an avatara, the other religious groups respect his nobility and moral courage. Thus Rama is an eternal national icon for all Indians.

Thus re-building Sri Rama Temple in Ayodhya becomes by consensus national goal. It must however be accomplished legally and with maximum consensus. This book is about how it can be accomplished. The re-building of the Rama Temple is part our renaissance. It means righting a historical atrocity. This book is written to educate our young patriotic generation about our true past and how to move forward. For this purpose the Virat Hindustan Sangam was founded on 14 September 2015.

SUBRAMANIAN SWAMY
President, Virat Hindustan Sangam

CONTENTS

I

India's National Identity and Sri Rama

Why is Sri Rama such a magnet for the Hindu masses, irrespective of caste or denomination? The question may puzzle some people who do not know our heritage since Sri Rama neither performed any miracle on his own, nor did he himself ever claim to be an *avatara* of Lord *Maha Vishnu*.

Nevertheless, it is significant for even the most lay observers that after so many millennia, the *Ramayana* is still evergreen in the minds of all true Indians; and Rama Lila is celebrated with gusto and rejoicing every year in every part of our nation.

Sri Rama and his associates immortalized in *Ramayana,* have endeared themselves to millions of people all over the world especially South and East Asia, transcending even religious barriers as the famous quote from Iqbal's poem that "Rama is *Imam e Hind,"* shows.

The awareness of the greatness of Sri Rama is not limited only to humans on earth. Even Hindu Gods have been quoted on his quality of being *Maryada Purushottam* There is for example a very enlightening dialogue between Lord Shiva and his spouse Parvati, which occurs in the concluding part of *Vishnu Sahasranamam* in the epic *Mahabharata.*

Vishnu Sahasranamam is a recital of the one thousand names of Lord Mahavishnu. Therein a conversation between Bhishma and Yudhistra is given. Yudhistra, had addressed the following questions to Bhishma: "Who is the one God? What is the supreme goal? What is the highest duty of the man? How can man reach the highest end of life?" To this Bhishma replied that the Supreme Being is omnipresent and therefore rightly called *Maha Vishnu,* and that His thousand names ward off all sin and fear. Then, in one hundred and seven stanzas, Bhishma recited the one thousand names of *Maha Vishnu* in succession.. Towards the very end Goddess Parvathi enquired of Lord Shiva, in the following *sloka*,

Kenopayena Laguna Vishnor Nama Sahasraham
Patyathe Pandithair Nithyam Srothumichamyaham Prabhoh:

(i.e "Does there exist any abridged version of this garland of one thousand names, which will have the same efficacy as reciting all the thousand names?").

To this, Lord Shiva replied to Parvathi as follows:

Rama Rama Ramethi, Rame Rame Mano Rame
Sahasra Nama Thattulyum Rama Nama Varanane:

(i.e. "the recital of just the one word 'Rama' will produce an effect equivalent to reciting all the thousand names of *Maha Vishnu*:")

Therefore, even gods and goddesses themselves felt the power and the charm of Sri Rama, hence why would it surprise anyone if ordinary mortals like us Hindus worship this Lord?

The worship of Sri Rama pervades not only India but many other countries in South-East Asia. For instance, in Thailand, there is a province called *Ayutthya* (Ayodhya), wherein about 75 kilometres north of Bangkok, there is a Rama temple.

According to historians, this *Ayutthya* bears testimony to Ram Rajya. Longstanding cultural contacts existed with the Kingdom of Thailand upto 1344 AD; and at that time King U-thong (*Uttanga* in Sanskrit) who ruled at a place called Nong Sano, named his capital *Ayutthya* after the capital city in India from which the Raghuvansi King Rama ruled. U-thong adopted his name as Ramathibodi, which in Sanskrit, means "the king under the empire of Rama." It is also said that Rama's son, Lava, visited *Ayutthya.* There are more than 400 temples of Rama and Sita in Thailand alone. This is not just a thing of the past. The most modern Bangkok international airport adorns paintings depicting scenes from the Ramayana.

Sikhs believe that their first two Gurus, Guru Nanak and Guru Angad Dev (both belonging to the Vedi clan) were descendants, in the seventeenth generation, of Lava, the elder of the twin sons of Sri Rama; while the other eight Gurus, namely, Guru Amardas, Guru Ramdas, Guru Arjun, Guru Hargobind, Guru Hari Rai, Guru Harikrishnah, Guru Teghbahadur, and Guru Gobind Singh (all belonging to the Sodi clan) were descendants of Kusha, the other son of Sri Rama.

Sikhs believe that just as Allah is the ultimate God for Muslims, so in their holy book, *Guru Grant Sahib*, Sri Rama is referred to as the Almighty One God. The name Rama occurs in more than 100 places in the holy book.

Some of the references are extracted below:

VILAVAL MAHALLA FIFTH. (Chand)
Aang Sri Guru Granth Sahib Ji 846

MALLAR MAHALLA FOURTH
Aang Sri Guru Granth Sahib Ji 1265-1266

SORATH MAHALLA NINTH

Aang Sri Guru Granth Sahib Ji 631

According to some Sikh scholars, just as Lord Rama is the *avatar* of Lord Maha Vishnu in the Treta Yug and Lord Krishna in the Dwapra Yug, Guru Gobind Singh is the avatar of Lord Maha Vishnu in the Kali Yug.

Other appreciations of and references to Sri Rama.

(a) Within India: The sheer divine beauty of Rama's personality inspired the poet Iqbal to declare him the 'Imam-E-Hind':

Hai Ram key wujood pey Hindostan ko naaz
Ahl-e-nazar samajhte hain usko Imam-e-Hind
Ejaaz ous chiraagh-e-hidaayet kaa hai yahee
Raushantar azsaher haizamane main sham-e-Hind.

In short, Ram is the spiritual head of India, even according to Iqbal, who was otherwise a devout Muslim.

It was largely the work of Tamil saints such as Alwars and Nayanmars that the depiction of Sri Rama evolved from that of a young prince of Ayodhya to that of a divine avatar. Hence Sri Rama symbolizes India's unity of North and South, just as Krishna unifies East and West.

(b) In China

Interestingly, a Chinese Ambassador to India Sun Yuxi told me that there has been an ongoing scholarly debate in China, about the origins of the Monkey-hero Sun Wukong in the Chinese epic novel *Xiyouji* viz., does his origin stem from Hanuman, or is Sun Wukong a product of indigenous Chinese folklore?

The theory of a possible connection between Sun Wukong and Hanuman was first mooted by Hu Shih, the well known poet and President of Beijing University. In 1936, at the Harvard University Tercentennial Celebrations, Dr. Hu delivered a seminal speech entitled "Indianisation of China." Therein he spoke disapprovingly of the Chinese people swallowing and digesting Hinduism in the garb of Mahayana Buddhism, and accepting idol worship. In its way, Dr. Hu's speech was as seminal as the nineteenth century Minute of Macaulay which resulted in a new trend of downplaying and attempting to obliterate all traces of India's native culture.

Like the Rama tradition in India ,its tradition in the *Xiyouji* (translated as *Journey to the West*) has had a profound impact upon Chinese society. The Xiyouji is one of the most popular and well-known novels in the canons of Chinese literature.

The Xiyouji epic is based on the real life journey of Xuanzang (Hsicung Tsang in India literature) also known by the Buddhist honorific *Tripitaka*. Xuanzang traveled to India along the overland route of the Silk Road. In this epic novel, Tripitaka (i.e. Xuanzang) is accompanied by four disciples: Sun Wukong, Zhu Bajie, Sha Heshang, and the Dragon Prince (the last appears in the form of a white horse). The novel begins with the birth and early years of Sun Wukong, the hero of the novel. The first six chapters, recount Sun Wukong's quest for immortality, his unruly behavior, and finally his capture and punishment. From Chapter Six to the end of the novel, the plot focuses on the birth of Tripitaka and his pilgrimage to Buddha's mountain, where he obtains certain sutras.

Unlike Southeast Asian civilization, Chinese civilization after the Ching dynasty (1642 to 1911) had begun to develop independently of India's cultural influence. This is not the case elsewhere in Asia; and thus the impact of Indian culture today is not as powerful in China as it is in Southeast Asia. Nevertheless, several elements of Chinese culture, including literature, were affected by the culture of Hindustan. [For an authoritative account thereof, see Dr. Hera S. Walker's "Indigenous or Foreign: A Look at the Origins of the Monkey Hero Sun Wukong," Sino-Platonic Papers, 81 (September 1998) [http://www.sino-platonic.org/abstracts/spp081_monkey.html].

(c) Elsewhere in Asia

Likewise, the Rama tradition is not only pervasive in India, but is known and studied throughout Southeast Asia. Throughout the whole of Asia, representations of monkey figures are depicted in oral narration, theater, art, and, in modem times, television shows. Shrines have been erected by devout worshippers to pay homage to them. Clearly, the popularity of these monkey heroes is without question.

There are hundreds of renditions of the Rama saga within India alone. The Ramayana of Valmiki, who is claimed by Dalits of India as their own, is reputed to be the most prestigious and the most comprehensive of all the renditions. Hanuman is the monkey-general of the Monkey-king Sugriva. By the king's command, Hanuman is ordered to aid Prince Rama, the central hero of the saga, in finding his captive wife, Sita, abducted by the demonic titan Ravana .Hanuman occupies a central role in the search and rescue of Sita. He is the one who finds Sita and leads the charge against the titan army to rescue her.

So how was the Rama tradition transmitted to Southeast Asia and China? Trade, more than any other factor, provided different civilizations with a vehicle for cultural exchange, motivating people to cross over mountains, deserts, and large bodies of water. Of all the civilizations that participated in long-distance trade across the Eurasian landmass and throughout the eastern oceans, India's was one of the most influential. In an overview of history it is easy to see the effect left by India's culture in the arts, statecraft, and religion of many Southeast Asian countries. For example, the early plastic arts of Cambodia, Thailand, and Malaysia exhibit a strong Indian flavor in their style and subject matter.

(d) Sri Lankan References

Very recently, in order to attract Indian tourists in a big way, the Sri Lanka Tourism Development Authority (SLTDA) has formed a committee to work out an ambitious scheme to develop and promote as many as 34 sites in the island associated with the Ramayana, as set out below.

Ravana had brought Sita to Sri Lanka in a flying machine called "Pushpaka Vimanam" by the Hindus and "Dandu Monara Yanthraya" by the Sinhalese Buddhists. This landed at Werangatota, about 10 km from Mahiyangana, east of the hill station of Nuwara Eliya in central Sri Lanka. Sita was then taken to Goorulupota, now known as Sitakotuwa, where Ravana's wife Mandodari lived. Seetakotuwa is about 10 km from Mahiyangana on the road to Kandy. There Sita was housed in a cave at Sita Eliya ,situated today on the highway that links Colombo with Nuwara Eliya. A temple dedicated to her exists there even today. Sita is believed to have had her bath in the mountain steam flowing beside this temple.

These are not the only sites in Sri Lanka associated with the Ramayana:

(a) North of Nuwara Eliya, in Matale district, is Yudhaganapitiya, where the Rama-Ravana battle is reputed to have taken place.

(b) Again ,according to a Sinhalese legend, Dunuwila is the place from where Rama shot the "Bramshira" arrow (Brahmastra) that killed Ravana.

(c) Ravana made his battle plans in a place called Lakgala. This is a rock from the top of which Ravana could see northern Sri Lanka clearly. It served as a watchtower following the expectation that Sri Rama would invade the island to rescue his Sita. It was at Lakgala that Sri Rama's killer arrow is said to have struck Ravana.

(d) Thereafter, the scriptures say, Ravana's body was placed on the rock at Yahangala for his subjects to pay their last respects; and this place is pointed out even today.

(e) Since Ravana was a Brahmin, it was considered a sin to kill him, even in battle. To wash off the sin, Sri Rama prayed at the Munneswaram temple in Chilaw, 80 km north of Colombo.

(f) At Manaweri, north of Chilaw, is the temple Sri Rama is said to have gifted.

(g) Rumassala and Ramboda, also in the tea-growing central highlands, are associated with Hanuman. It is believed that Hanuman dropped the Dronagiri mountain, which he brought from the Himalayas, at Rumassala. At Ramboda, known for its massive waterfalls, a temple for Hanuman has sprung up. Legend has it that the Koneswaram temple, in the eastern district of Trincomalee, was a gift to Ravana from Shiva.

The documents available in Sri Lanka state that at the Buddha Vihara at Kelani, near Colombo, there is a representation of Rama handing over the "captured" Sri Lanka to Ravana's brother Vibheeshana, who sided with him in his conflict with Ravana.

SYNOPSIS AND CRITIQUE OF ALL THE ABOVE

It is therefore completely false to propagate, as DMK leader Karunanidhi has been doing, that Sri Rama is merely a North Indian God. There are historical evidences aplenty to show that the worship of Sri Rama as a divinity, took birth and evolved in the South, the 'Dravida' country, *and later got assimilated into the religious psyche of the North*. There are also inscriptional evidences to dismiss the attempt to link the rise of the worship of Sri Rama to the 'Islamic' invasion of North India in the 12th-13th centuries.

In her S.C. Misra Memorial Lecture entitled "The Making of a Hegemonic Tradition: The Cult of Rama Dasarathi," delivered at the 67th Session of the Indian History Congress, where she was later elected as President, Professor Suvira Jaiswal said that it was possible to "trace the gradual emergence of a full-fledged Rama cult in the Dravida country." The Vaishnavite saints of the south, the Alwars sang in praise of the local cult-spots as sanctified by the presence of their favourite deities. This gave scope for the identification of various places as scenes of events associated with the characters of Ramayana and celebration of the existing temples as that of Sri Rama.

Clear evidence of the setting up of shrines to Sri Rama as an incarnation of Vishnu, was available from the 10th century onwards in the Chola and Pandya kingdoms, which had been the locale of Alwar activities, Professor Jaiswal said.

Although the Chola kings were worshippers of Siva and constructed magnificent Siva temples, several of them assumed titles suggestive of their identification with Rama. For instance, Aditya Chola (AD 871-907), who claimed to have built several Siva temples on the banks of the Cauvery, assumed the title

'Kodandarama.' His son Paranthaka I called himself Samgraama Raghavam, i.e; Rama in battle.

In the Ananda Ramayanam, the commencement of the construction of the dam is described as follows: "Rama, who hails from Raghu Dynasty, installed the idol of Lord Vinayaka after giving directions about the dam to Nala. Then Rama worshipped the nine stones installed by Nala, representing the nine planets. This can be seen even today on the way from Ramanathapuram to Mandappam. He then conveyed his willingness to Hanuman about installing a wonderful linga in his name where the three seas meet. It is this area that Adi Sankara described as 'Dravida' to Mandana Mishra.

"The mountain like dam 'Nalasethu' was built on the orders of Rama" says Vyasa in his Mahabharatha [3.267.45]

REFERENCES TO RAMA IN THE PURANAS

The *Bhagavatha Puranam* says that Balarama went to the dam "which can purify even the greatest sins" .i.e. 'Samudhram Se Mahamath Mahapataka Nasanam,' [10th Skandam-Sarukkam 79]

The *Padma Puranam* says, "this sethu was built by me within three days with the help of Vanara Sena." [Srusti kandam-Sarukkam 38]

The Skanda Purana says "the mere vision of Rama Sethu will relieve one from Samsara bandhas." [Sethu Mahatmiya Kandam-Sarukkam 1]

Thus, the Puranas say that the dam Sethu was built in the middle of the sea by Rama and ordain that it is a holy spot.

REFERENCES TO THE RAMA SETU IN TAMIL LITERATURE

There is a reference to the Sethu in the Tamil Sangam classic, Akananuru, where a comparison is made between the uproar that occurred in a certain village clash, and "the sound heard from the sea near Thriuvanaikkarai (Adi Sethu), in Pandya Kingdom which was built by Rama, the great warrior."

In his Pasurappadi Ramayanam, Periyavaccan Pillai, one of the Vaishnava Acharyas, writes

"Malaiyal Anaikatti Marukarai eri."

'Sethu Puranam' also known as 'Sethu Mahatmiyam' is a Sangam era classic which contains 45 Sarukkas and 3438 verses, written by Niramba Alagiya Singar in the 16th Century. Recently it has been verified by Nallur Arumuga Navalar of Jaffna and published by Chidambaram Saivapprakasa Vidyasala Dharmaparipalakas.

Sri Ponnusamy Thevar of Ramanathapuram Samasthanam took up the effort to publish this work to which Sodashavadanam Subbiraya Chettiyar, a deciple of Tiricirapuram Mahavidvan Meenatchisundaram Pillai has contributed the 'Sirappuppayiram.' In that, he has sung praises of the Sethu described as—'Titara oduum Sethu Manmiyatthai.'

Another poet Kumarasami Pillai has referred to 'Sethumanyamana vadanul thannai.' In the prayer song of 'Sethu Puranam' the dam built by Sri Rama has been mentioned as "Tuya Seer Ramasethu."

The Sethu's greatness and its sanctity has also been sung of in 64 verses in the chapter 'Sethu Sarukkkam.' The need to built the Sethu for Sri Rama has been explained in 'Sethu Vanda Sarrukkam.' In 151 verses of the 'Sethu Madhava Sarukkam' and 'Sethu Yatthirai Sarukkam,' are detailed the benefits reaped by merely thinking about the Sethu and taking a holy dip in it. The Tala Puranam (Volume I) in Tamil literature also mentions the 'Sethu puranam.'

It remained a traditional practice of Tamils to give lectures in praise of 'Sethu Puranam.' Arumuga Navalar, who was one among those who did so, has also written it in manuscripts. It was printed and published by Sri M.R.M.S. Ramalinga Pillai of Rameshwaram in the name of 'Sethu Makattuvam' (Rameshwara Manmiyam). This 'Sethu Puranaprasangam' which begins with Suta Puran (a narration of the story to Sounakadi Rishis in Naimisaranyanm) is written in the form of a dialogue.

"Anaiyalai Sulkadal Andradainadu Vazhiseithavan" says Thiru Gnana Sambandar in his Tevaram. TRANSLATE

Thirunavukkarasar in his Tevaram sings of the construction of the dam by Sri Rama as "Kadalidai Malaikal Tammal Adaittu Mal Karumam Muttri." TRANSLATE

All the above references from epics puranas and literature— written in different languages, in different times stand testimony to the fact that the dam 'Sethu' was built as per the orders given by Sri Rama to Nala.

SETHU NADU

The Samashthana of Ramanathapuram (Ramnad) was called as 'Sethu Nadu' only because of the very existence of the 'Sethu.' The King of this samashthana was known as Sethupati and Sethu Kavalar [i.e. Lord of the Cause way]. Thirupullani which is 6 miles southeast of 'Ramnad' is known as Adisethu. Ramayana says Sri Rama appointed people from the Maravar community to protect the 'Sethu' and the people who come to take a holy bath in it.

All the kings of this dynasty are called as 'Sethupati' by the people of successive generations One of the kings of 'Sethupati dynasty' constructed a town near 'Thirupullani.' It was named as "Mugavai" as it stood at the gateway to the 'Sethu.' Later it became Ramanathapuram.

It is obvious that the kings of Sethu Nad had long cherished connection with the Sethu. Among them, Adiraghunatha Sethupati, Jeyatunga Raghunatha Sethupathi,Ativeera Rahunatha Sethupati Varaguna Raghunatha Sethupati and six others are mentioned as the earliest kings of the Sethupati dynasty.

The names 'Rahunatha' and 'Sethupati' are attached to them, because of their relationship with Sri Rama [Who is also called Raghunatha] and the dam built by him. It stands as a clear testimony to the existence of Rama Sethu and also to the point that all the kings of the 'Sethupati' dynasty ruled this area with great devotion and dedication.

RECENT REFERENCES TO RAMA SETU

In 1910 Ramanathapuram district was constituted. The Manual about its political, geographical, industrial, agricultural, economical growth, besides information about population its distribution, transport, revenue, ports, holy places after several revisions was updated in 1968. and was released only in 1972, after making some necessary final changes.

The Foreword to the District Manual of Ramanathapuram was written by the then Chief Minister of Tamilnadu, M. Karunanidhi. He observed:

> "The task of collecting and publishing the district manuals was given top priority after independence and was given preference in the five year plans. The District Manual of today is not only a guide furnishing mere information. It is

of great help containing several important topics and *can be used very much as a source of great reference. A manual throws light on our age and traditions and long cherished culture*. It serves as mirror which reflects our society. Once having a thorough knowledge of the Manual we can march forward keeping our head high and be proud of our well nurtured culture and traditions."

Skanda Purana (VI.101.1-44) describes the installation of three Shiva linga at the end, middle and beginning of Rama Setu is described. This is also related in *Kurma Purana* (21.10-61).

Garuda Purana (1.811.-22) listes sacred placed including Setubandh and Rameswar. Narada Purana (Uttara Bhag 76.1-20), extols the greatness of Rama-Setu.

In *Encyclopedia Brittanica*, it is stated thus: Adam's Bridge also called Rama's Bridge, is a chain of shoals, between the island of Mannar, off northwestern Sri Lanka, and Rameswaram, off the southeastern coast of India. Traditionally, it is said to be the remnant of a huge causeway constructed by Rama, the hero of the Hindu epic Ramayana, to facilitate the passage of his army from India to Ceylon (Sri Lanka) for the rescue of his abducted wife, Sita. According to Muslim legend, Adam crossed there to Adam's Peak, Ceylon, atop which he stood repentant on one foot for 1,000 years (http://www.britannicaindia.com/duk_det_inside.asp?art_id=28)

According to late V. Sundaram IAS (Retd.) and a prolific writer, Lord Pentland, the then Governor of Madras, in 1914 wrote to the Viceroy Lord Hardinge that "I would earnestly request you to direct the Archeological Survey India (ASI) to undertake an extensive and intensive survey of Rameswaram and it's beautiful environs, particularly with reference to the historic and primordial Adam's Bridge."

This request was never acted upon. Even after India became free from foreign rule, the Rama Setu continued to be neglected. The Ministry of Culture in 2007 went so far as to deny the need to carry out a survey at all to determine whether the Rama Setu qualified under law to be declared an 'Ancient Monument.'

There are of course scientific and other evidence to prove that the Rama Setu is an ancient land-bridge that was constructed and hence should be declared as a World Heritage Monument.

USA's NASA, and NRSA of the Ministry of Space, Government of India satellite photo images clearly establish a causeway—like formation between Dhanushkodi in India and Talaimannar island in Srilanka. Of course, the NASA is in no position to state whether the formation is natural or constructed.

It was wrong for the government to interpret this inability, to claim that it was indeed a natural formation! The bridge is composed of a series of islands and shoals (sand accumulations created by ocean currents). Thus, the entire bridge right from the sea-bed to the surface sea level is a bridge formation which has been recognized for long as a land bridge linking the two regions: Bharatam and Srilanka.

To what extent there was manual intervention in connecting the gaps between the shoals and islands during the pre-historic periods as detailed in the ancient texts such as Ramayanam is a matter for detailed marine archaeological and geological evaluation.

The reports of submergence of Kumarikandam, Poompuhar, Dwaraka along the coastline and the formation of the Gulf of Khambat about 10,000 years ago (confirmed by scientists of National Institute of Ocean Technology) point to the possibility that the recent historical record of submergence of Dhanushkodi island should provide pause and re-evaluation of the impact of the ocean currents and changes in sea-level on the coastline and also on the SSCP.

Such a multi-disciplinary archaeological-geological-aquatic environment study should be undertaken respecting the sentiments of the people who have looked upon the bridge as a land-link between Bharatam and Srilanka.

The fact that India is described in the Government seal as *Aasetu himachala paryantam,* the fact that the project itself is called Setusamudram canal project (Setu means bridge), confirms the tradition related to the bridge. Hurting the sentiments of the people who revere Sri Rama as a divinity and personification of dharma, will be a serious breach of trust and will evince utter disdain for peoples' sentiments. Thus the pros-and-cons of reactivating the land bridge between Srilanka and Bharatam should be considered afresh.

According to S. Badrinarayanan Director (Retd.), Geological Survey of India his investigations reveal that the Rama Setu is not a natural formation but a constructed causeway.

Earlier most of the arguments are based on assumptions and partial data obtained from NASA satellite images. No doubt these images are astounding as they bring out the marine geomorphology of the area, but as stated by NASA official themselves "Remote sensing images from orbit cannot provide direct information about the origin or age of a chain of island, and cannot determine whether humans were involved in producing any of the patterns seen."

The observations of Dr. Badrinarayanan were based purely on hard field work including geological and geophysical surveys coupled with logging and interpretations of several cores and boreholes carried out in the area. A considerable amount of geological information is now available.

The earth has not always been very warm or cold. There have been periods of extreme cold climate that occurred in the geological past wherein most of the surface of the earth was covered with vast quantities of ice and these periods are referred to as Ice Age. The recent one occurred during the late Pleistocene age eighteen thousand years before present. During this period the sea level was lowered by about 130m than what is today. Due to this the land area was extending far greater distances than what is today. The Indian subcontinent was extending far beyond Sri Lanka. Subsequently due to global warming and other causes there have been periodic rises in sea level submerging several of these additional areas. About 7300 BP there was a major spurt in sea level rise which resulted in submergence of several areas all over the world.

The Indian side of the land mass adjoining the Ramsetu originates from the southeastern end of the Rameswaram Island. The island itself is a long linear sandy terrain providing calcareous sand stone and occasional coral formation. This area was devastated by a major cyclone in 1956 when part of the area was lost to the sea. The Rameswaram Island connects the main land through the Pamban area. Further to the west charnocites and granites are exposed.

In order to understand the geology and the structure of the area in the marine domain, several surveys were carried out onboard a research vessel with underwater sensor. These included multibeam echo sounder survey, sub bottom profiler survey, side scan sonar and magnetic survey. The entire area was sampled by deploying vibro core, mainly to the north of the Ramsetu. These surveys generally required at least 4m of water surface so that the equipments are not damaged. The bathymetric survey brought out the fact that the bridge, with a shallow ridge varying in width from 1.6 to 4 km. This part of the area could not be surveyed due to these factors. However it was seen from the geological and geophysical surveys that the Bridge is a fault zone rising suddenly from the Bay of Bengal side to the north. This scarp like feature is the shallowest part of the Rama Setu. Even though it is mostly submerged in water there are series of small Islet like features which project above the sea surface. In all about 10 boreholes have been drilled along this ridge up to the international boundary. Out of the ten boreholes, six boreholes were in the sea. The result of the bore logging clearly showed about 1.5m to 4m marine sand followed by 1.5 to 2.5 m of boulders of calcareous sand stones and coral followed again by marine sand to various depths end at continuous compact formation.[see Figure 4].

It is a well known fact that the coral reefs can only form in clean and unpolluted water and these being marine organisms required firm and compact formation as foundation. The presence of loose marine sand below these clearly indicates that these are not natural and are transported. Unless somebody has transported and dumped them these could not have come there. Some of the boulders arc so light_they could float on water. Apparently whoever has done it has identified it as light and strong boulders to make it easy for transportation. Since the boulders are strong they can withstand lot of weight.

There are corals that are present on land in Rameswaram, Pamban and Tuticorin areas. A study of them and dating them clearly show that the age of the coral is about 10,000 years and the sea level at the time was 4m above the present day sea level. Then there has been a lowering of sea level and between 4 to 5 thousand years BP the sea level was about 1.5 m above present day sea level.

The 1.5 to 2.5 m thick zone of corals and rock presently occurring at shallow depths in the sea atop the crustal portion of the Adams Bridge appeared to be an ancient causeway. The ancients appeared to have taken advantage of the crustal portion of the ridge to avoid dumping of lot of volume of rocks and boulders and also utilized less dense but compact rocks and boulders so that these could be carried easily to greater distances and at the same time strong enough to withstand pressure from above both by human as well as sea forces.

The Rama Setu is a wonderful divide separating the turbulent Bay of Bengal in the north and the calm and tranquil waters of Gulf of Mannar to the south. Due to this tranquil condition, very rare species of corals and other sea organisms grew in the Gulf of Mannar, whereas the species are completely absent in the Bay of Bengal side. The turbulent tide and the associated sediments caused by the severe cyclone that occur every year in the Bay of Bengal are prevented by the ridge of the Adams bridge and there by protect the delicate conditions in the Gulf of Mannar.

The dredging and opening of the Setu in all likelihood may cause the sediments and turbulent tide to enter the tranquil Gulf of Mannar and choke and destroy the delicate coral island. As an alternative dredging in the Pamban or nearby areas and by passing the Rama Setu hence be favourably considered like other inter sea canal e.g., Panama Canal. Locks could be provided both in the palk bay side and Gulf of Mannar side so that such calamities could be prevented.

Based on this evidence, I wrote to the Ministry of Culture demanding an inquiry, but for some mysterious unreasonableness the Minister declined to consider the demand.

Besides Dr. Badrinarayanan, the Earth Sciences Department of the Union Government in an opinion sent on a reference from the then President of India Dr. Abdul Kalam (and reported in the Kolkata daily *The Telegraph* of May 8, 2007) stated the same view as follows:

> "During the glacial Maxima, the sea level was about 130 m lower than what is today. This is evidenced both on the east and west coast of India, where submerged Corals occur around 1 to 2 m water depths and they are clear indicators of near coastal zone.... However, during the last ice age (18,000 year BP) the entire area from India to Sri Lanka and further south and southeast were contagious land due to the highly lowered sea level. As and when there were major melting of glaciers both from the mountains as well as from the Antarctic area, the sea level was rising. These features were well recorded and studied by several submerged Coral formations all over the world. About 7,300 years BP the sea level in the southern part of India was about 3.5 m above the present level. This has been deciphered by Dr. P.K. Banerjee, who studied Corals that found in the land part as of Pamban, Rameswaram, and Tuticorin etc. Subsequently the sea level went down and rose +2m above than what is today between 5000 to 4000 years B.P. In almost of all the boreholes between 4.5 and 7.5 m the borehole intersected hard formations, which have been found to be calcareous sand stones and corals. It is to

be pointed out here that Corals are comparatively less dense, compact and somewhat easy to carry. The Corals normally grow atop compact to hard formations for the purpose of stability, and as the sea level rises, the Coral colony grows up vertically to maintain water depth of 1 to 2 m, which is essential for their survival. It is always observed that these Corals have continuous vertical growth like Lakshadweep, Andaman's, and Gulf of Mannar Natural Park. These have always been found to grow on hard rock bottom. In the case of Adams bridge area we observe that the Coral formations hardly occur 1 to 2.5 m in length and resting on loose marine sands. Most of these coral rock pieces are seem to be rounded pebbles of corals. *These things appear to point these coral rock pieces and pebbles have been transported and placed in these areas*. Since the calcareous sand stones and Corals are less dense than normal hard rock and quite compact, probably these were used by the ancients to form a connecting link to Sri Lanka, on the higher elevations of the Adams bridge ridge and this is analogous to modern day causeway. In support of these observations there are many archaeological and geoarchaeological evidences on the south east coast of India around Rameswaram, Tuticorin and the western coast of Sri Lanka. There are raised Teri formations that supported a rich assemblage of mesolithic— microlithic tools indicating the presence of strong human habitation and activity in these areas as early as 8000 to 9000 years B.P and as recent as 4000 years B.P. On Sri Lanka side there are indications of human habitation extending to late Pleistocene (about 13,000 B.P) based on bone and fossils of human and animal form. All these point to a flourishing human activity on both side of Adams Bridge and probably when the sea levels were just right the link between India and Sri Lanka could have been established."

Eminent Archeologist former DG ASI late Dr. S. R. Rao also wrote to the Union Minister of Shipping to opine that the Rama Setu was constructed and not natural formation.

Thus as the then Tamil Nadu Chief Minister Karunanidhi, and his ilk have been telling outright lies to the public about the non existence of the Rama Setu, and lauding on the economic and environmental viability of the Sethusamudram Shipping Channel Project (SSCP) disregarding the sentiments of the Hindus.

While Karunanidhi as CM in his speeches had debunked the Setu and Rama, the DMK State, and the UPA Union, Governments had at the same time been advertising and affirming the exact opposite: existence of the Setu and the historicity of Rama to attract Hindu pilgrims and tourists!

For example, the Tourist Department of the TN Government has been advertizing in Railway trains, urging the people to visit Rameshwaram and see where Rama set his "lotus feet," to build a bridge (Setu) to Sri Lanka with the help of the Vanar Sena (see enclosed photo), to rescue his wife Sita.

The National Remote Sensing Agency (NRSA), of the Union Ministry of Space has published a book of satellite photographs [ISBN: 817525 6524] claiming that "archeological studies show" that the Setu may be "man made." This book has been distributed to all MPs free by the Ministry of Space. Yet Ms. Ambika Soni as the then Minister of Culture to a question in Rajya Sabha (August 14, 2007) falsely stated that "no archeological studies have been made in respect of the Rama Setu."

The Ministry of Environment and Forests had in a letter dated April 8, 1999 to the Ministry of Surface Transport, conveyed it's opinion that the SSCP should be scrapped as it is an environmental disaster (see Annexure 5). This opinion was based on an analysis of the NEERI Report of 1998. Yet in 2004 the Ministry reversed it's opinion based on the same 1998 data. Why? No explanation has been given so far for this somersault. This is the extant to which UPA went to deny the existence of Sri Rama and the episodes of Ramayana.

The Ministry has also suppressed as stated earlier above a report prepared by Dr. S. Badrinarayanan, former Director of Geological Survey of India (GSI) in which based on a 2002 investigation under the sea near and at the Setu. The Report concluded that Rama Setu had been constructed, at least 9000 years ago, and is not a natural formation as claimed by the then union government.

Yet without consulting the GSI, the Ministry of Culture hastily filed an affidavit in the Supreme Court that "there is no information or studies in the knowledge of the Government that Rama Setu is man made." Former ASI DG S.R. Rao had also ridiculed this stand government. Fortunately, the BJP Government today is slowly rectifying the past historical fallacies. Union Shipping Minister Shri Nitin Gadkari has categorically declared to Parliament that Rama Setu would be never touched even if Sethusamudran Shipping Project (SSCP) is cleared for implementation on environment grounds. Minister of Culture Shri Mahesh Sharma has set into motion the papers to declare Rama Setu as a National Heritage Monument, and the path Rama took from Ayodhya to Lanka repaired and musuems set up wherever Rama, Sita (upto Nasik) and Lakshmana stayed.

II

The Historicity and Heritage of Sri Rama

Yet after all these citations, the English-enslaved mindset of certain contemporary intellectuals of India refuses to accept the historicity of Sri Rama : to such persons the Ramayana and the Mahabharatha are merely 'mythology.'

In 1813, James Mill and. Charles Grant from the East India Company's Haileybury College, wrote the book "History of India" wherein they classified most of the literature of India as 'mythological.' Thereafter the Indian tutees in an Anglo-Indian educational system operated in English medium ,just repeated this appellation like trained parrots. Mill and Grant classified these texts as mythological on the following premises:

1. The events described in these texts seem to have occurred before the date of creation of the earth (fixed by Father James Usher at 9 AM on 23rd Oct, 4004 BCE). Hence, it was argued, these texts which describe India and the existence of its civilization prior to this time could not be real and must be mythical or imaginary.

But of course Father Usher has now been proven wrong by modern cosmology and traditional archeological finds. Hence this premise of Mill and Grant is without basis.

2. Basing themselves on self-serving Greek texts, the eighteenth and nineteenth century British historians held that Alexander defeated Porus in 326 BCE and that it was he who

had spread Greek culture and thereby civilized India and that until then Indians were uncivilized barbarians. But the civilization described in the Ramayana and Mahabharatha texts (both predating Alexander) seemed to be advanced in science, technology, culture, philosophy and linguistics. Hence, it was argued, they could not have existed prior to the arrival of Alexander and hence the texts must be mythical.

But thereafter, not only has the existence of a civilized India prior to the arrival of Alexander, been proved beyond doubt, but also the talk of the defeat of Porus at the hands of Alexander is now being questioned: after all it is certain that Alexander turned back after reaching the Indus—which he was unlikely to have done had he been victorious.

Certainly too, no reference to Alexander survives in contemporary Indian texts, so it does not appear that Alexander created any sort of impression—let alone a deep cultural impression—on the India of his days. Hence this premise of Mill and Grant is also baseless.

3. The British came up with the concept of the 'Aryan Invasion of India' (which is stated to have occurred around 1500 BC), which spread its culture and civilized Indians who until then were uncivilized barbarians. Hence, again, it was argued that the civilization described in these texts, which seemed to be more advanced in science, technology, culture, philosophy and linguistics could not have existed prior to the Aryan Invasion and hence the texts must be mythical.

But today, the idea of an Aryan Invasion has been dismissed even by Western historians as a figment of imagination and a concoction by the British imperialists to justify their occupation of India: their argument being that they (i.e. the British), are as legitimate occupiers of Indian territory and as legitimate beneficiaries of India's natural resources as foreigners of the Aryan race, who had invaded and settled in India and supplanted the original inhabitants of the Dravidian race.

This Aryan—Dravidian classification has now been proven to be racially incorrect: modern DNA analysis has determined that despite their differences in features and complexion (which differences are now traced to local factors, temperatures and pigmentation), most Indians belongs to the same race.

Also the study of traditional Indian texts has brought to light how the terminology 'Dravidian' was based on geographical division and was not racial, cultural or civilizational. The various Indian languages have a common Sanskrit vocabulary of upwards of 40 percent and they also have a similar syntax; and all their scripts have evolved from Brahmi. Thus this premise of Mill and Grant is likewise fatally flawed.

4. Mill and Grant also held that the texts were mutually inconsistent and hence the texts must be imaginary or mythical. It is to be noted that while the texts are alleged to be inconsistent, nevertheless British historians and their Indian tutees have uncritically accepted the genealogy in the Puranas. (Otherwise, for example, how do historians of all schools, Western and Indian, know that Ashoka was the son of Bindusara or that Samudragupta was the son of Chandragupta Gupta, or that the Maurya dynasty succeeded the Nandas?) Given this, gaps or inconsistencies in narration cannot detract from the historicity of the texts. We cannot accept a part but not the whole, after reconciling the apparent inconsistency.

Thus, it is submitted, all the premises of Mill and Grant for classifying Indian literature as mythological are flawed.

Much to the consternation of—or perhaps rnvy as well of—British trained historians, there is no other civilization as ancient and continuous as India.

THE ESTABLISHED TEXTUAL EVIDENCE OF RAMA

Valmiki, the author of the original Ramayana text was a contemporary of Sri Rama. This has been explicitly stated in the text itself. This story was not penned a few hundred years after Sri Rama. In fact, Valmiki was the guardian of the wife and sons of Sri Rama. Thus the Valmiki Ramayana has all the credibility attached to a contemporary historical account. If we look at various historical texts the world over, we find that authors have generally written about stories which happened a few hundred or even a few thousand years prior to their times. In such historical texts, the authenticity and the exactness of the material can be questioned.

Ramayana being a popular story of India, many authors down the centuries have written their own versions of Ramayana. Kalidasa, the great Sanskrit poet of the 5th century CE wrote his *Raghuvamsa,* his poem on Sri Rama and his forebears. The Tamil poet Kamban wrote his version of Kamba Ramayana over 1000 years back. Goswami Tulsidas wrote *Ram Charita Manas* in the 17th century. These three and many other eminent authors across India have penned the story eulogising Sri Rama and emphasizing his divinity.

The Puranas of India also mention the details of the story of Sri Rama. The stories mentioned in the Puranic texts and the original Ramayana of Valmiki cross validate each other in many places. This adds further credibility to the Valmiki Ramayana text being rightly termed as *Itihaasa* (i.e., "it thus happened"), a historical text.

VALIDATION BY PLACE NAMES

Dr. Ram Avatar spent 25 years in researching whether the locations described in the Ramayana can be located in modern

India. In particular, he was able to locate and photograph many of the spots through which Sri Rama traveled on his journey from Ayodhya to Sri Lanka (see Figure 3) and he has documented these with photographs in his monograph *Jahan Jahan Ram Charan Chali Jayi* ("Wherever the Footsteps of Rama fell"), published in 2007.

SKY CHARTING OR ARCHEO-ASTRONOMY

Planetarium software is a tool that, given a date in future or past and vice-versa, helps to arrive at planetary positions i.e. given a set of planetary configurations, one can arrive at the dates on which such configurations occurred, either in the future or in the past. There are probably over 50 different software available for this purpose. Each software can be used specifically for a particular application, like plotting the current night sky chart, predicting eclipses and the like. The person who has pioneered research on the topic is Shri D.K. Hari of Bharath Gyan.

When a spacecraft is launched for a journey to far-off planets like Jupiter or Saturn, its travel time would be well over 12 years. The software helps determine orbital positions of the planets when the spacecraft reaches their orbits. Naturally then, a high level of precision is required in the software.

Unlike that of any other civilization so far, it is a characteristic of the literature of the Indian civilization that there are innumerable accounts where some event is recounted along with night sky observations of the time of that event. By feeding the observations of the planetary configurations into the planetarium software, we can obtain the English calendar dates when these configurations could have occurred in the past.

When these dates are logically arranged along with the events, it helps us to scientifically assign dates to events mentioned in Indian legends and historical texts, and thus it goes a long way towards validating them.

This would be particularly true where there are no inconsistencies in such correlation of event and night sky configuration. In fact, it would be a stupendous and scientifically acceptable method of dating such event. A whole new and valid methodology of dating ancient events emerges, with exciting possibilities.

Thus the astronomical data left behind in our literature can be analysed scientifically to arrive at historic dates for various events. This approach is parallel to archaeology where physical remains are analysed to arrive at historic dates: it gives rise to a new branch of scientific dating which may be called Archaeo-astronomy. Many Indian researchers have made use of this software to arrive at historic dates for various events described in the literature. They have collated the outputs of such work that are worthy of scrutiny. (It should be made clear that the planetary combinations occur cyclically in time. Hence the same planetary combination could be seen not just in the present Yug but also for example in the Treta Yuga i.e., 17,50,000 years ago. This is the only weakness in this calculation; and it has been unscrupulously used by Western researchers to sneer at ancient Indian history: on the argument that human events could not have credibly occurred 17,50,000 years ago).

The works of Pushkar Bhatnagar, on the Historicity of Sri Rama form the basis of what is presented here to know the possible dates of the events in Sri Rama's lifetime.

Historical Dates of Sri Rama

Events of Sri Rama	Date
Sri Ram Navami – Birthday	January 10, 5114 BCE
Birth of Bharatha	January 11, 5114 BCE
Pre-coronation eve	January 4, 5089 BCE
Khar, Dushan episode	October 7, 5077 BCE
Vali Vadham	April 3, 5076 BCE
Hanuman's Visit to Lanka	September 12, 5076 BCE
Hanuman's Return from Lanka	September 14, 5076 BCE
Army march to Lanka	September 20, 5076 BCE

Source: Bhatnagar, Pushkar: Dating the Era of Lord Ram.

The dates arrived at for the events in Table 2 above tally with the chronological sequence for the events as found in the Ramayana text: in fact the elapsed time between the events as indicated by these dates tallies with the elapse-time and their duration/age as described in the Ramayana. But (as pointed out in the last paragraph) the problem with this calculation is that planetary configuration is cyclic in time. This same configuration would occur once every 7122 years, and hence we need more evidence before we can rule out Tretayuga or confirm the above dates.

RAMA SETU DEPICTIONS IN VALMIKI'S RAMAYANA

In his Ramayana, Maharshi Valmiki has described the construction of the 'Setu' known to the nation for several millennia as 'Rama Setu'; and to the British, since the 19th century, as 'Adams Bridge.' The Ramayana states that this was built in a record time of 5 days under the leadership of Nala, the son of Viswakarma; that in Treta Yuga, following the advice of Samudraraja (who picked the site for Sri Rama, to thank Sri

Rama for having saved him from the Lord's ire), Sri Rama asked Nala to construct a dam on the sea to Srilanka; that Nala agreed, and under his direction, the Vanaras went in all directions and brought coral rocks, stones, trees, cut or uprooted, and built the 48 kilometre long and 3 kilometre wide causeway-like structure to enable Sri Rama's army to walk across to Sri Lanka.

The *vanara* sena uprooted rocks which are stated to resemble "huge elephants," using machines and they brought them to the sea shore with the help of carrier vehicles. "The dam constructed by Nala who was as skilled and talented as his illustrious father, resembled the milky way," says Valmiki. "The joyous roar raised by the vanaras on completion of the dam silenced even the deadliest noise of the mighty ocean." [Sarukkam 22, sloka 51-75]

In another verse, (this occurs in the 'Yuddha Kanda' of Adyatma Ramayanam), Valmiki recites the words of Sri Rama returning with Sita in a Pushpaka Vimana as follows: "Here is the Sethubandhana worshipped by three worlds. It is a holy place. It has the ability to relieve all the greatest of sins. It was here that Mahadeva [Lord Siva] extended his whole hearted support to me earlier." [*Yuddha Kandam* – 126.20.1].

About the actual construction of the Rama Setu, various stanzas of the Valmiki Ramayana give minute, graphic and marvelously evocative details. Thus:

> "At Rama's command, those lions among the monkeys entered the mighty forest with alacrity in hundreds and thousands on every side and those leaders of the simian tribes, tearing up the rocks, which in size they resembled, and the trees also dragged them to the sea and they covered

the ocean with Sala, Ashvararna, (list of tree names). Those foremost monkeys transported those trees, with or without roots, bearing them like so many standards of Indra (the king of heaven) and they heaped (list of tree names) here and there. With the aid of mechanical devices, those powerful colossi dug up stones as big as elephants and rocks, and the water suddenly spouted into the air only to fall instantly. Thereafter those monkeys churned up the sea by rushing into it on all sides pulling on the chains."

"That immense causeway constructed by Nala in the bosom of the sea was built by the arms of those monkeys of formidable exploits and it extended over a hundred leagues."

"Some brought trunks of trees and others set them up; it was by hundreds and thousands that those monkeys, like unto giants, made use of reeds, logs and blossoming trees to construct that bridge, rushing hither and thither with blocks of stone resembling mountains or the peaks of crags, which, flung into the sea, fell with a resounding crash."

"The first day those monkeys resembling elephants, of immense energy, full of high spirits and exceedingly merry, erected fourteen leagues of masonry. The second day, those highly active monkeys of formidable stature set up twenty leagues. Bestirring themselves, those giants threw twenty-one leagues of structure over the ocean on the third day and on the fourth, working feverishly, they built up twenty-two leagues in extent. The fifth day, those monkeys, industrious workers, reached to twenty-three leagues distance from the further shore."

"That fortunate and valiant son of Vishvakarma (architect of the demigods), leader of the monkeys, constructed a causeway worthy of his sire over the ocean and that bridge erected by Nala over the sea, the haunt of whales, dazzling in its perfection and splendor, was like the constellation of Svati in space."

"Then the gods, Gandharvas, Siddhas (living beings superior to humans) and supreme Rishis (great sages) assembled in the sky, eager to see that masterpiece, and the gods and Gandharvas gazed on that causeway, so difficult of construction, that was ten leagues in width and a hundred in length built by Nala."

"Those monkeys thereafter dived, swam and shouted at the sight of that unimaginable marvel that was almost inconceivable and caused one to tremble! And all beings beheld that causeway thrown over the ocean and by hundreds and thousands of kotis (millions), those monkeys, full of valor, having built that bridge over the immense repository of waters, reached the opposite shore."

"Vast, well-constructed, magnificent with its wonderful paved floor, solidly cemented, that great causeway like unto a line traced on the waves, resembled the parting of a woman's hair."

"Meanwhile Vibishana (brother of Ravana who joined Rama), mace (club) in hand, held himself ready at his post with his companions in case of an enemy attack. Thereafter Sugriva addressed Rama, who was valiant by nature, saying Mount on the shoulders of Hanuman; and Laxmana (brother of Rama) mount on those of Angada. O Hero, vast is this ocean, the abode of whales; those two monkeys who freely range the sky will transport you both."

"Then the fortunate Rama and Laxmana advanced thus and that magnanimous archer was accompanied by

Sugriva. Some monkeys strode forward in the center, some threw themselves into the waves, some sprang into the sky, others marched on the bridge, some ranged through space like birds, and the terrific tumult of the trampling of that formidable army of monkeys drowned the roar of the ocean."

"When those simian troops had passed over the sea by the grace of Nala's causeway, the king ordered them to camp on the shore which abounded in roots, fruits and water."

"At the sight of that masterpiece that had materialized under the command of Raghava (another name of Lord Rama), despite the difficulties, the gods, who had drawn near with the Siddhas and Charanas as also the great Rishis, anointed Rama in secret there, with water form the sea, and said: "Mayest thou be victorious over thy foes, 0 Thou, who are a God among men! Do Thou rule over the earth and the sea eternally! "

"Thus in various auspicious words, did they acclaim Rama in the midst of the homage offered to him by the Brahmins."

(From *the Ramayana* of Valmiki, Yuddha Kanda in Chapter 66: "The Great Causeway")

Thus, according to Valmiki, was constructed the great causeway Rama Sethu. It survived as a causeway for several millennia; and it remained in use into recent historical times. Even as recently as 1478 A.D, it was known to be in use as a footbridge cum causeway to cross over from India to Srilanka. It is this Rama Setu, described above, that we see even today from Dhanushkodi across to Talaimanar in Sri Lanka [see: Satellite photo imaging by NASA & ISRO]. It is this sacred

Setu that the Government today wants demolished in the name of building a channel furrowed out of the shallow ocean floor in the Palk Straits.

True and devout Hindus believe that Bhagvan Sri Rama was born in Ayodhya, the then capital of a flourishing kingdom of the Suryavamsa dynasty. Rama is venerated as *Maryada Purushottam*, and worshipped by Hindus of the north. As an *avatar* of Vishnu, while it was first propagated by the Tamil saints known as Nayanmars and Alwars who composed many hymns and songs dedicated to his divinity, the North which later came to accept Rama as one, especially thanks to the saint Tulsidas, the fervor for Rama worship is much more. In that sense, Sri Rama was the first truly national king of India, supra region, supra varna or jati. That is why poet Iqbal called him 'Imam-e-Hind.'

The exact spot of the palace where Rama was born has been and remains firmly identified in the Hindu mind and is held as sacred. This is the very area where stood from 1528 till December 6, 1992 a structure that came to be known as Babri Masjid, put up in 1528 by Babar's commander Mir Baqi.

In fact, Baqi was a Shia Muslim, and hence he intended it to be a place for Shias to read namaz. Today, interestingly, it is the Sunni Wakf Board, which entered the legal dispute as late as 1961, that has been litigating in the court claiming the title to the land on which the structure once stood.

I call it a "structure" since it cannot be strictly called a mosque by Sunni edicts—because it did not have the mandatory minarets and *wazu* [water pool]. Moreover, Islamic scholars and clerics uphold the Muslim countries governments to demolish or shift mosques for construction of roads and houses. (Annexure No. A-4 to A-6) That a Ram temple existed and or that there is a sacred spot known as Ramjanmabhoomi is attested by many ancient sources and by modern scientific methods.

In Skanda Purana [Chapter X, Vaishnav Khand] the site is vividly described. Valmiki Ramayana also describes it beautifully. Less than two decades before Mir Baqi carried out the horrible demolition of the Ram Temple, Guru Nanak had visited the Ramjanmabhoomi and had darshan of Ramlala in the mandir at the spot.

There are many commentaries on this visit which are a part of the Sikh scriptures. Guru Nanak himself records the barbarity of Babar's invasions [in Guru Granth Sahib at p. 418]. In Akbar's time, Abul Fazal wrote the Ain-i-Akbari in which he describes Ayodhya fame as the place of "Ram Chandra's residence which in Treta age combined spiritual supremacy and Kingship" [Tranlated by Col. H.S. Jarrett and published in Kolkata in 1891].

In Chapter X of the Report of the Archeological Survey of India, NW and Oudh (1889), it is mentioned (p.67) that Babri Mosque "was built in AD 1528 by Mir Khan on the very spot where the old temple of Janmasthan of Ram Chandra was standing."

III

The Legal Arguments for Building the Ram Temple

Mark Twain had once said that "It is a lot easier to mislead the people than convince them that they are misled." This is the reality about the Ram Temple in Ayodhya, the reality about which I wish to bring to nation's attention.

People in India have been misled to believe that a temple and a masjid are both equally revered religious places. This misconception is at the root of our failure so far to negative and through consensus and re-build and or restore the Ram Temple in Ayodhya, the Krishna Temple in Mathura, and Vishvanath Temple in Varanasi.

The fundamental reality is: A masjid is not, in Indian case law, or international case law, or even under the Sharia jurisprudence (which is the law for Muslims), held to be religiously sacred. It is considered a prayer hall to read 'namaz' and congregate for the same. Even airports have such prayer halls in some countries. The Supreme Court Constitutional Bench in Faruqui vs Union of India [(1994) 6 SCC 376] has held that a mosque is not an essential part of Islamic religion (para 82), and that namaz can be read anywhere [Annexure No. A-3].

This is the position in Islamic law as propounded by scholars in Saudi Arabia, in which country the authorities demolish mosques to lay roads, build parks or multi-storied apart buildings. Even the mosque in Mecca where Prophet Mohammed used to read namaz, was demolished for a new building and road to pass through!

On December 6, 1992, a super structure called the Babri Masjid standing in the city of Ayodhya, came crashing down. It was an unauthorized demolition and an outcome of mob violence. There is a criminal case in courts on this issue.

It remains even today a traumatic event for the nation, because the so-called secular Indians have been weaned on a untrue and contrived history of India, and hence a large section of our educated class still view the destruction of the structure as criminal vandalism.

If it was not criminal vandalism, then what was it? The demolition of the original temple to build a mosque was the real act of vandalism. There it was a state directed deliberate vandalism to overawe the Hindu population. Babri Mosque was demolished by a mob and it was criminal destruction because it was unauthorized by law.

Two years earlier before the demolition, by a coincidence, on the same month and day, I had met representatives of the VHP and BJP at a house, next door to mine, on Mathura Road.

The newly sworn in Prime Minister Chandrashekhar had asked me [I was then his newly sworn in senior most Cabinet Minister] that as the new Union Law and Justice Minister, I should talk to them about withdrawing their proposed massive nation-wide stir slated to begin on December 9, 1991 for building a Ram temple at the site the super-structure had then stood in its gloomy glory.

Chandrashekhar told me to assure the VHP that our government would get removed the Babri Masjid with the consent of Muslim leaders through discussions on the above stated principles.

The VHP and BJP leaders I met readily agreed to call off the stir since we were a new government, while the stir decision was taken when V.P. Singh was PM.

Thereafter in January 1991 talks began, initiated by Chandrashekhar himself with the Muslim leaders. Unfortunately, despite the zig-zag progress in the talks, our government did not last long enough to fructify it. The near unanimous opinion was we would find out an amicable settlement with 12 months.

Had instead the government lasted for a year more, I am confident we would have amicably liberated the Ranjanmabhoomi for building a befitting Ram temple, and with the consent of the Muslim community, even though the Government was in the minority in the Parliament.

From my personal experience as a Minister in a minority government, I can therefore say that lack of majority in Parliament is no excuse for implementing any agenda, if the leadership had the mindset to get things done.

As a Minister of Law and Justice, for instance, I made the controversial Sessions Judge of Faizabad, K.M. Pandey a High Court judge, despite the fact that the previous V.P. Singh's "three-legged" government had issued orders on file that since Pandey had directed the locks on the so-called Babri Masjid be removed in 1986, he should never be made a High Court judge.

Mulayam Singh was our Chief Minister of UP, but with firmness I however got his protests sufficiently moderated so that he permitted me to go ahead. He cooperated because he knew I would do it anyway—make Pandey a judge of the High Court—and hence he acquiesced since he wanted other things done for him by me. In those, there was no collegium of judges to decide. The Law Minister was the final arbiter. Judges recommended, but sending to the President was a decision the Law Minister took subject to Prime Minister's approval.

The same clarity enabled the Chandrashekhar government to get Saifuddin Soz's kidnapped daughter freed without releasing any dreaded terrorists. There are methods for doing that—mostly based on retaliation. But it is still an official secret.

In each case it is the mindset of those elected to high office that matters, not the size of the parliamentary majority or lack of it.

It was this mindset that enabled the Chandrashekhar government to nearly solve by an agreement the question of building of a Ram temple in Ayodhya. The government however fell before it could be clinched.

But could the Babri Masjid be demolished or shifted to another site in a legally authorized way to make way for the Ramjanmabhoomi temple construction? Are not a temple and masjid once build be equally immutably sacred?

The fundamental question before us thus is this: Can a temple and a masjid be considered on par as far as sacredness in religious theology is concerned? Relying on two important court judgments I hold that today, the answer is: No!

Hindu temples constructed according to the Agama Shastra and after Prana Prathista Puja is the abode of the God whose idol is installed and that God to the owner of the temple. A mosque is essentially a prayer hall for namaz. And namaz can be done anywhere. Thus in Islamic countries that function under Sharia law, mosques are demolished or shifted for making way for roads and apartment buildings and the like.

A masjid is also *not* an essential part of Islam, according to a majority judgment of a Constitution Bench of India's Supreme Court.

In the famous Ismail Farooqui vs Union of India case [reported in [see (1994) 6 SCC360 at page 416 paras 80 to 86], the Supreme Court observed the presumption of sacredness and the house of God status of a mosque as follows: "It has been contended that a mosque enjoys a particular position in Muslim law and once a mosque is established and prayers are offered in such a mosque, the same remains for all time to come a property of Allah ... and any person professing Islamic faith can offer prayer in such a mosque, and even if the structure is demolished, the place remains the same where namaz can be offered" [para 80].

The Constitution Bench rebutted this contention stating: "The correct position may be summarized thus: Under Mohammed law applicable in India, the title to a mosque can be lost by adverse possession.... A mosque is not an essential part of the practice of the religion of Islam and *namaz* (prayer) can be offered anywhere, even in the open. Accordingly, its acquisition is not prohibited by the provisions in the Constitution of India." [para 82].

Thus, any Government depriving the Muslims of the Babri Masjid by an order of acquisition is within law, if the government decides to do so in the interest of public order, public health and morality [the reasonable restrictions enumerated in Article 25 of the Constitution].

The position in Islamic law is in fact even more clear: in Saudi Arabia the authorities demolish mosque to lay roads and build apartment building. Even the mosque where Islam's Prophet Mohammed used to pray was demolished!

Saudi Arabia, Pakistan, and even in British undivided India, masjids have been demolished mosques to build roads. Saudi Arabia even demolished the Bilal Masjid in Mecca where

Prophet Muhammed used to read namaz [see ANNEXURE No. 2].

Masjid, like Churches are not religious places in the sense a temple is. Masjids and Churches are places for worship, i.e., buildings which serve as facilitation centres for namaz and prayer. Namaz can be read anywhere even on a railway platform. In USA, VHP buys disused Churches and converts them into temples, and yet no Christian there objects.

But temples, once it is shown that prana prathista puja was performed to build it, is where God or deity resides, and belongs to God forever. There are many court judgments to support this view.

When I was Union Law and Justice Minister, this question of the status of a temple—even if in ruins or without worship—had come up before us in a case of a smuggled-out bronze Nataraja statue which was up for auction in London.

Earlier the Government of India, when Rajiv Gandhi was PM, had decided to file a case in the London trial court in 1986 for recovery. The Nataraja statue had by then been traced to a temple in ruins in Pathur, in Thanjavur district. A farmer named Ramamoorthi had in 1976 had accidently unearthed it while digging mud with a spade near his hut.

When the news spread, touts of an antique dealer by name Ahmed Hussein reached him and paid a small sum and smuggled it out to London, where in 1982 they sold it to Bumper Development Corporation Private Limited. In turn the said Corporation sent it to the British Museum for appraisal and possible purchase. By then the Government of India was onto it and asked the UK government to take action.

The Nataraja idol was seized by London Metropolitan Police, and thus the Bumper Development Corporation sued the Police in court for recovery but lost the case. An appeal was filed in the Queens Bench [i.e., our High Court level] which was dismissed on April, 17 1989. So, the Bumper Corporation went to the House of Lords [our Supreme Court level]. By then I had become Union Law and Justice Minister and seniourmost Minister. On February 13, 1991 when I was Law Minister, the judgment came, which is truly landmark, dismissing Bumper's final appeal [see (1991) 4 All ER 638].

The House of Lords upheld the Indian government's position that because of the *prana prathista puja*, a temple is owned by the deity, in this case Lord Shiva, and any Hindu can litigate on behalf of the deity as a defacto trustee. The Bench consisting of Justices Purchas, Nourse and Leggatt concluded: "We therefore hold that the temple is acceptable as party to these proceedings and that it is as such entitled to sue for the recovery of the Nataraja." [page 648 para g].

Thus, even if a temple is in ruins as the ASI had found the Thanjavur temple or destroyed, as Ram Temple was in the Babri Masjid area, any Hindu can sue on behalf of Lord Rama in court for recovery!

No such ruling exists for a mosque for the simple reason that a mosque is just a facilitation centre for reading namaz, and has no essentiality for Islam religion. It can be demolished and/or shifted as any building can and are being so today in Arab countries and Pakistan.

That is, the Ram Temple on Ramjanmabhoomi on the basis of the concept of inalienable sacredness has a superior claim to the site than any mosque. *This the fundamental truth in the Ayodhya dispute. This truth will apply, for example, to Kashi Vishvanath and Brindavan temple and other sites as well.*

Therefore under law the Union Government can acquire the Babri Masjid site by a public notification, and urge the

Muslim community to agree to shift the building of a new masjid to some other site well beyond and across the Saryu River.

It is important to note here that as of now there are eight mosques in Ayodhya area which the ASI has taken over since these had no one coming to read namaz. Hence what use will another mosque be?

Hence the national response to the judgment of Lucknow Bench of the Allahabad High Court allotting one-third of the Ramjanmabhoomi to the Sunni Wakf Board to build a mosque in the area near the Ramlala temple should be a resounding "No"!

A temple cannot be equated to a mosque in either its immutability or its divinity. The masjid in Islamic law is just a prayer hall building to facilitate reading of namaz, which anyway can be read anywhere. That is the legal position in all Islamic nations following the Sharia.

As Union Law and Justice Minister in 1991 I got our government legal team to prove this proposition to the satisfaction of the House of Lords in Britain, to bring back a Nataraja statue taken from a disused Thanjavur temple. It was at Rajiv Gandhi's request I took interest in the case.

But on the other hand, a Government can remove in a legal and orderly way the masjids in Ayodhya, Kashi, and Brindavan, in fact other 3000 places too, to rebuild the original temples under law. We can get Muslim population's cooperation in this even if those with property interests such as the Waqf Boards do not cooperate. I am confident of this.

Of course, because of this fact about masjids and churches, no one in a democracy can take law into his own hands to demolish these masjids and churches. Nor will the Hindu public wait forever for re-building the Sri Rama Temple in the Ayodhya *janmabhoomi*.

Hindus throughout foreign occupation of India have deeply and unwaveringly held as sacred that exact spot where the Babri Masjid once stood, as is recorded in many official and judicial proceedings.

In 1885, for example, Mahant Raghubar Das in a Suit No 61/280 of 1885 filed in the Court of the Faizabad Sub-Judge against the Secretary of State for India (who was based in London), prayed for permission to build a temple on the chabutra outside the mosque. His suit was dismissed on March 18, 1886.

However, in his Order the Sub-Judge, an Englishman, stated thus: "It is most unfortunate that a Masjid should have been built on land specially held sacred by the Hindus. But as the event occurred 358 years ago, it is too late now to remedy the grievance." Since the English as policy never sought to disturb the social status quo in India as evidenced, for example, on the 'Sati' question, the Judge took the easy way out and dismissed the Suit.

It is now well established by GPRS-directed excavations done under the Allahabad High Court monitoring and verification in 2002-03, that a large temple did exist below where that Babri Masjid structure once stood. Inscriptions found during excavations describe it as a temple of Vishnu Hari who had killed the demon king Dasanan [Ravana].

The Sunni Wakf Board does not accept these findings as of any meaning or of any consequences. It does not however matter if all this was indeed so or not, since under Section 295 of the Indian Penal Code [IPC] it is prescribed that "Whoever destroys, damages or defiles any place of worship, or any object *held sacred by any class of persons,* with the intention of thereby insulting the religion of any class of persons or with the knowledge *that any class of persons is likely to consider such destruction, damage or defilement as an insult to their religion,* shall be punishable with imprisonment of either description for a term which may extend to two years, or with fine, or with both."

That is, an offence under criminal law is committed if a body of persons hold something as sacred. It does not matter if the majority does or does not hold so. Nor can a court decide what is sacred and what is not. Only a body of persons can identify what is sacred. The offence under Section 295 IPC is cognizable and non-bailable, as well as non-compoundable.

Nor can we Hindus by the back door allow aggression and atrocity of demolishing temples be rewarded in any manner. Therefore, as with the Shah Bano case precedent, Government should bring an amendment to the *Acquisition of Certain Areas of Ayodhya Act* of 1993 to bar constructing any structure other than those connected with a temple for Sri Rama.

That will be the fit atonement of the so-called secular people of our nation for tacitly tolerating for so long the demolition of Ram Temple on the orders of Babar of Afghanistan. Babri, after whom the mosque is named incidentally was a 9 year boy in Kabul who was a "special" intimate of Babar with whom he was infatuate.

If such an amendment is not brought forth, Hindus should wage a fierce democratic struggle to force the government to do so.

Babri Masjid was built as an affront to Hindus. Otherwise it could have been built anywhere else since namaz can be offered anywhere. Hindus have however prevailed because despite 800 years of Islamic and 200 years of Christian domination, Bharat today is still over 80% of Hindus in population, and a continuing Hindu civilization.

Hence, now we must resolve to rectify what is essential to rectify and reclaim. For that restoration of three holy sites, in Ayodhya, Vrindavan, and Kashi. For these three, we patriotic politicians must resolve: *Come our way or go the highway*. Or as Savarkar said: "With you if possible; without you if not possible; but be clear, inspite of you if you oppose."

But we cannot prevail in this struggle, if we have in our midst those suffering from the "Arjuna virus" as—the late Swami Chinmayananda once pointed out, referring to Arjuna's initially declining to fight at Kurukshetra because he could recognize his duty in the hour of crisis. Babri Masjid legacy is that virus we still have to cure twenty years later.

In the Affidavit filed by the Government of India before the Constitutional Bench of the Supreme Court in the above cited 1994 Farouqi case judgment, the re-building commitment of the Government of India was recorded by the said Constitutional Bench in its judgment.

On pages 427-28 of the said Faruqui Constitutional Bench judgement of the Supreme Court judgment, the Solicitor General is quoted by the Supreme Court Constitutional Bench as stating on affidavit [filed on the direction of the Apex Court], as follows: "If ... a Hindu temple /structure did exist prior to the construction of the demolished [Babri Masjid] structure, government action will be in support of the wishes of the Hindu community."

This is also the similar commitment made in 1991 by the Muslim representatives of the Babri Masjid Action Committee to the Government when I as Union Law and Justice Minister was asked by Prime Minister Chandrashekhar, in November

1990, find ways to make the VHP withdraw its Kar Seva call scheduled from December 9, 1990 and to negotiate a settlement.

Subsequently prominent Muslim leaders made the following commitment: "... if these assertions were proved, the Muslims would voluntarily hand over the disputed shrine to the Hindus...." This commitment/assurance is recorded in Government of India's *White Paper* [in paras 2.1, 2.2, and 2.3].

Thereafter, Chandrashekhar arbitrated for a negotiated settlement, which included demolishing the Babri Masjid, re-building the Ram Temple, and building new masjid for the Shia community across the Saryu River.

It may be kept in mind that Mir Baqi, Babar's commander, was a Shia and the Babri Masjid that he constructed was for the Shias. The hereditary Muthwali [supervisor] today is also a Shia and he is, I am reliably told, agreeable to re-building a Ram Temple in Ayodhya site, and a masjid across the Saryu River.

"Most importantly, the ruling BJP party now in the Union Government has committed in its 2014 Manifesto to building a Ram Temple at the Ayodhya site if it is legal to do so."

Is it so? It is now obvious that it is undoubtedly legal to do so under the existing case laws, which reason is bolstered by the nature of a masjid being a mere prayer hall under the Sharia Islamic law, the assurance given by the Muslim community leaders to the Janata Party government led by Chandrashekhar, and recorded in the White Paper issued by the Union Government, and is a solemn sworn commitment of the Government of India made to the Supreme Court.

ROAD MAP

Therefore, what should be the road map or blueprint for our government to deliver on the 2014 Manifesto promise? The following steps may be taken by 2016 to re-build the Ram Temple in Ayodhya and fulfill our commitment to the electorate:

(i) Appoint a former Chief Justice of India, such as for CJI S.H. Kapadia as the Executor. The office of the Executor may liaise with a designated Minister such as General V.K. Singh.

(ii) The designated Minister may issue Notice to the Babri Masjid Muthwali who is a hereditary supervisor, and is living in India, asking him to formally agree to withdraw his claim to the Ramjanmabhoomi, and offer him an alternative site for a masjid to be built at public expense, across the Saryu river.

(iii) Call a meeting of Islamic clerics, Indian and foreign, and seek their endorsement. The Supreme Court may then be approached for disposing off all pending SLPs and Writ Petitions.

(iv) If such an endorsement is not forthcoming then the Government should move an enabling Bill in Parliament and have it passed.

(v) Create a Ram Temple Re-Building Committee on the Somnath temple model, with Shri Ashok Singhal of VHP as Chairperson.

(vi) Begin construction of the Ram Temple on an auspicious date in 2016.

But in the meantime there is no need to torture and humiliate the bhaktas and devotees who come to worship at the present makeshift Ramlala Mandir. They get no basic facilities of drinking water, shoe/chappal racks, toilets and parking spaces. Yet a whopping entry fee is collected from the devotees.

The question is whether these restrictions are violative of the fundamental rights of worship under Article 25 of the Constitution, subject of course to reasonable restrictions of public order, health and morality, and also of fundamental right to hygiene [AIR 1952 SC 196 & AIR 1999 SC 92]

This Hon'ble Court [in the Farooqui case:(1994) 6 SCC 361] had permitted worship in the makeshift temple of Ramlala, subject to maintaining the *status quo* in the disputed site.

But what is the scope of this direction to maintain status quo is, has also been made clear by this Hon'ble Court [(1994) 6 SCC 361 at 394], i.e., the *mandate* given to the Receiver in Section 7(2) of the Acquisition of Certain Areas at Ayodhya Act [1993] to ensure that *status quo* as of January 3, 1993 in the disputed *area* is maintained. The area of dispute has been defined with clarity in the aforesaid judgment in para 24 on page 395.

But in the name of maintaining the status quo, the Receiver and the UP administration have imposed the most unreasonable and arbitrary restrictions on the worship itself, tantamount to sacrilege, and causes gross inconvenience to the lakhs of devotees coming from all over India for darshan.

That whether the present restrictions are beyond this Hon'ble Court's mandate was gone into by a Special Bench of three Hon'ble judges of the Allahabad High Court on the Writ Petition No. 3067 of 1994 filed by D.N. Agarwal, praying for modification of unreasonable and arbitrary restrictions on devotees placed by the Receiver on the access to, and worship of the Ramlala idol at the temple in the disputed area.

The Hon'ble High Court while allowing the Writ Petition, passed an order [vide Order dated February 23, 1996] detailing the various necessary modifications in the restrictions. This was stayed by this Hon'ble Court on a petition filed not by the Receiver, but by an interlocutor in Syed Hashmi in1996. I have challenged this by way an Interlocutory Application [IA].

The issue in this IA thus arises from this stay or injunction granted by this Hon'ble Court in 1996, and which injunction is continuing till date.

In my affidavit I have therefore prayed that the injunction on the directions of the Allahabad High Court Special Bench be vacated because the present restrictions imposed by the Receiver are arbitrary, unreasonable, oppressive and violative of Article 25 of the Constitution. In fact even the Hon'ble High Court observed that the Receiver implicitly admitted the same.

In a nutshell, it is an admitted fact that there is a makeshift Ramlala Mandir, on the site of the Ram Chabutra which site was for centuries inside the perimeter of the now demolished Babri mosque.

This Hon'ble Court had [vide (1994) 6 SCC 361] appointed a Receiver for the disputed area but permitted the continued worship at this temple, subject to maintaining status quo as of January 3, 1993.

In the name of the status quo, the appointment receiver has imposed restrictions on the access to the temple and the mode of worship.

The Hon'ble three judge Bench of the Allahabad High Court, after hear a Writ Petition, passed a detailed Order in February 1996 holding these restrictions as arbitrary and unreasonable, and directed the Receiver to implement restrictions which the Hon'ble Bench stated to be reasonable.

While the Receiver did not appeal against that Order, an intervenor filed in 1996 filed a SLP and got an ad interim injunction which continues today. No proceedings thereafter till I revived the issue by way of an IA in 2009.

The question is whether the restrictions on worship and access imposed by the Receiver bear any nexus to the scope of status quo in the area of dispute, and whether these restrictions are violative of the fundamental rights of worship under Article 25 of the Constitution, subject of course to reasonable restrictions of public order, health and morality, and also of fundamental right to hygiene.

What the scope of this direction to maintain status quo is, has also been made clear by this Hon'ble Court [(1994) 6 SCC 361 at 394], i.e., the *mandate* given to the Receiver in Section 7(2) of the Acquisition of Certain Areas at Ayodhya Act [1993] to ensure that *status quo* as of January 3, 1993 in the disputed *area* is maintained. The area of dispute has been defined with clarity in the aforesaid judgment in para 24 on page 395.

IV

Concluding Comments

The relationship of fundamental rights with the Directive Principles of State Policy in Part IV of the Constitution has been a subject of considerable and continuing debate. A division of fundamental rights into two categories—justiciable and non-justiciable—was recommended by the Sapru Committee as early as 1945. At the time of framing the Constitution, the Advisory Committee on Fundamental Rights recommended:

> "We have come to the conclusion that in addition to these fundamental rights, the Constitution should include certain directives of State Policy which, though not cognizable in any court of law, should be regarded as fundamental in the governance of the country."

Directive principles are not enforceable by any court but the principles laid down are, nevertheless, fundamental to the governance of the country and it is the duty of the State to apply these principles in making laws (Article 37). Part IV prescribes the goals or the ideals to be achieved by India as a Welfare State. Fundamental rights are the means for realizing these goals.

At one stage there was a sharp controversy regarding the role of fundamental rights vis-a-vis directive principles. Early judicial thinking took the view that directive principles were subsidiary or subordinate to fundamental rights.

The Constitution also prescribes the rights and duties of a citizen and it is the responsibility of the State to ensure the citizen gets his rights, as also encouraged to perform his duties as a part of the soft infrastructure of good governance.

The structure of our Constitution is consistent with the Hindu tradition, a part of Hindutva. Ancient Bharat or Hindustan was of *janapadas* and monarchs. But it was unitary in the sense that the concept of *chakravartin* [propounded by Chanakya], i.e., of a *sarvocch pramukh or chakravarti* prevailed in emergencies and war, while in normal times the regional kings always deferred to a national class of sages and *sanyasis* for making laws and policies, and acted according to their advice. This is equivalent to Art.356 of the Constitution.

In that fundamental sense, while Hindu India may have been a union of kingdoms, it was fundamentally not a monarchy but a Republic. In a monarchy, the King made the laws and rendered justice, as also made policy but in Hindu tradition the king acted much as the President does in today's Indian Republic. The monarch acted always according the wishes and decisions of the court-based advisers, mostly prominent sages or Brahmins. Thus Hindu India was always a Republic, and except for the reign of Ashoka, never a monarchy. Nations thus make Constitutions but Constitutions do not constitute nations.

Because India's Constitution today is unitary with subsidiary federal principles for regional aspirations, and the judiciary and courts are national, therefore the Rajendra Prasad-monitored and Ambedkar-steered Constitution—making, was a continuation of the Hindu tradition. *This is the second pillar of constitutionality for us—the Hindutva essence*! These aspects were known to us as our *Smritis*. Therefore, it is appropriate here to explore ways by which Hindutva can be blend into the present Constitution more explicitly.

The framers of the Constitution of India also seemed to be aware of the Hindu heritage of India. A perusal of the final copy of the Constitution, which was adopted by the Constituent Assembly on November 26, 1949, is most instructive in this regard. The Constitution includes twenty-two illustrations within its main body. These illustrations are listed at the beginning of the Constitution. The illustrations are apparently chosen to represent various periods and eras of Indian history.

These illustrations have been selected to represent the ethos and values of India, which the Constitution seeks to achieve through its written words. The framers of the Constitution appear to have had no doubt in their minds that the Hindu heritage of this country is the ballast on which the spirit of the Constitution sails.

The emphasis of these illustrations is on those symbols that encapsulate the most significant and authentic moments of a nation's history. The personality of Shri Rama, the enunciation of the Gita by Shri Krishna, the valour, humility and service of Shri Hanuman, the teachings of Bhagwan Buddha and Mahavira, the emphasis on academic pursuits symbolized by the Gurukul and the University of Nalanda. These images may not be said to exhaust the Hindu heritage, but they do capture the essential concerns of the Hindu mind: struggle against the evil forces, dedication to duty without passionate attachment, service and humility, compassion and charity, highest importance attached to learning and academic attainments, freedom to hold diverse opinions and view points and an uncompromising spiritual eclecticism. These are the virtues that the Constitution seeks to visually represent and legally enforce without favour and fear. The Constitution, it was intended, to represent Hindu ethos.

The illustrations selected to represent the 'Muslim' period also imply this intention: Only two illustrations have been selected: (i) A portrait of Akbar and (ii) portraits of Shivaji and Guru Gobind Singh.

From the whole range of Muslim themes, only Akbar is selected. Akbar come closest in his ideals and practices to what can be called the Hindu spirit: his relatively liberal politics, his reported refusal to make the Mughal state an instrument of exclusive Muslim hegemony, his relatively less hostile attitude towards Hindu religion, his refusal to treat Hindus as degraded dhimmies on account of religious belief. Akbar approximated to a certain extent the Hindu ideal of social and political behaviour and unsurprisingly found a place in the Constitution of India.

The other two men who represent the 'Muslim Period' are Shivaji and Guru Gobind Singh: men who fought the persecution and bigotry of the Mughal rule under the successors of Akbar, especially Aurangzeb. Akbar is chosen because he was liberal: Shivaji and Gobind Singh are chosen because they fought the oppression and cruelty of the Mughal state which was acting as the instrument of Islamic religious supremacy. They refused to recognize a political dispensation that functioned as an instrument for the fulfillment of Islamic religious agendas. They fought for safeguarding the dignity of their culture and religious values from the depredations of a theocratic Muslim state. The three represent the grand spiritual if secular, ethos of Hindutva. *The Constitution of India is cognizant of this fact.*

The pictures chosem from the British period and the era of India's freedom movement are also unique. The former era is represented by Tipu Sultan and Rani Lakshmi Bai, both inveterate warriors against European colonial domination, warriors whose battles were not defined in terms of mere speeches and slogans but enacted within the context of blood and sweat. Another figure chosen from the phase called 'Revolutionary movement for freedom' is Netaji Subhash Chandra Bose. One is compelled to ask the question: Why is Netaji chosen to represent the revolutionary movement for the freedom of India? The fact is that it was Netaji whose gallantry and dedication raised the morale of the freedom fighters and led to wider repercussion in other sections of Indian society. His courage, his sacrifice, his fighting spirit are the true values representative of the final assault of the Indian people on the edifice of colonial rule. The only person chosen to represent the theme 'India's Freedom Movement' is Mahatma Gandhi, whose deep association with Hindu values, Hind Swaraj and Ram Rajya are no hidden facts. The Constitution of India thus seems to have chosen very Hindu icons to represent its ethos.

The 'aroma' of Hinduness or Hindutva also permeates the most important constitutional and administrative units of the Indian state. Nowhere is it more apparent than in the august premises of the Indian Parliament—a house where matters of national concern are discussed and the fate of the nation is decided. The head of the Lok Sabha is the Speaker, and what we find inscribed holdly above the Chair of the speaker is the following: *Dharmachakra Pravartanaya* (for the turning of the wheel of righteousness). It is accepted by all that the notion of 'Dharma' is the most significant cultural signifier of the Hindu world. The rulers of ancient India had accepted the path of dharma as their area of political exertion and the managers of free India's politics accepted that notion by putting the *dharamachakra* on the national flag, and the related motto in the central place of the highest legislative body.

The Parliament of India bears prominent reminders of the Hindu ethos at many places:

(i) At door no. 1 is inscribed –

Lok Devarampatraarnu
Pashyema tvam vayam vera

(Chhandogya)

Open the door for the welfare of the people and show them the path of noble sovereignty.

(ii) At the door of the Central Hall –

Ayam nijah paroveti ganana laghuchetasam
Udarcharitanam tu vasudhaiva kutumbakam

(Panchantantra)

To think in terms of 'me' and 'others' in a narrow say; for the men of liberal character the whole world is one family.

(iii) On the dome near lift no. 1 –

Na sa sabhayata na santi vriddhah
Vriddhah na to ye na vadantidharmam
Dharmah sa no yatra na satyamasti
Satyamna tadyachhalambhyupaiti

(Mahabharat)

No assembly is a sabha which does not comprise elders; he is not an elder who does not speak according to dharma; no dharma survives without truthfulness; and every truth is necessarily devoid of cunning and deceit.

(iv) On the dome near lift no. 2 –

Sabha v na praveshtaya
Vakavyam va samanjasam
Abruvan vibruvan vapi
Naro bluvati kilvishi

(Manusmriti)

"Either do not enter the sabha or speak only according to dharma when you are inside it. Those who do not speak or speak untruthfully and unrighteously are partakers of sin."

These teachings—and there are many more—inscribed on the domes and walls of the Indian Parliament signify the values that the fathers of Indian democracy and parliamentarianism wanted to inculcate. It goes without saying that all the noble virtues included in the above mentioned aphorisms are derived from the Hindu heritage of India. The founding fathers seem to have found a deep consonance between India's Hindu ideals and the ideals of a modern secular democracy.

The impact of Hindu heritage and its value systems on the legal and administrative life of India becomes all the more apparent when one examines the core ideals adopted by various institutions. Some of the examples are as follows:

(i) Government of India - *Satyameva Jayate*
(ii) Lok Sabha - *Dharmachakra Pravartanaya*
(iii) Supreme Court - *Yato Dharmastato Jayah*
(iv) All India Radio – *Bahujanhitaya*
(v) Doordarshan - *Satyam Shivam Sundaram*
(vi) Indian Army - *Seva Asmakam Dharmah*
(vii) Indian Navy - *Shan No Varunah*
(viii) Indian Air Force - *Nabhah Sprisham Diptam*
(ix) Delhi University - *Nistha Dhriti Satyam*
(x) Life Insurance Corporation of India - *Yogakshemam Vahamyaham*

These ideals are ideals of the Hindu world. They do not convey religious dogmas, therefore no rituals or gods are invoked in them; they are civilisational values whose sanction comes from deep humanism and a commitment to a righteous way of life. They are noble virtues whose adoption was deemed to be relevant for the future of modern India's democratic polity. The Indian Constitution and the Indian polity pay their homage to the ancient value systems of the Hindu way of life, and Hindutva.

Thus the interpretations of the higher judiciary of the land, assigning the Hindu way or Hindutva to the centuries old socio-cultural underpinnings of India are not an exercise of mere juristic interpretation. It is more fundamentally the acknowledgement of those social, cultural, ideational and political norms that give the people and territory of India their defining identity.

Inspite of the currently fashionable denial by the purveyors of a warped secularism, the Hindu underpinning of India's milieu have been vested with great significance by the leaders of the freedom movement and has been subtly but insistently stated in the structures of the democratic institutions set up by Independent India. Our Constitution, our Parliament, our highest Judiciary, and other important organs of the state recognize most clearly that the ultimate normative sources of inspiration for shaping free India's destiny would remain the millennia old heritage of Hindu ideals and civilisational concerns.

The founding fathers of India's political regime seem to have no doubt in their minds that India can remain a pluralistic and democratic polity only to the extent that it adheres to the fundamental values of a democratic, polyform and pluralistic Hindutva.

So the question arises: Will Hindutva be a contradiction or violative of the Constitution? In other words, can Hindutva be incorporated by amending the present Constitution subject to the Basic Structure Rule? I find from my research that most major Hindutva goals do meet the test of Constitutionality and hence need to be pursued even under the present Constitution. Of the decisions of the Supreme Court commonly referred to as the "Hindutva decisions," the most important one is in *Manohar Joshi* [(1996)1 SCC 169].

In his election speeches Manohar Joshi, the winning Shiv Sena candidate had said that "[T]he first Hindu State will be established in Maharashtra." The High Court of Bombay set aside his election. But the Supreme Court restored Joshi's election observing that "a mere statement that the first Hindu State will be established in Maharashtra is by itself not an appeal for votes on the ground of his religion but the expression, at best, of such a hope."

The Court went much further and using the words "Hindu," "Hinduism" and "Hindutva" interchangeably observed that those terms were not amenable to any precise definition and no meaning in the abstract *would confine the term "Hindutva" to the narrow limits of religion alone*. The Court further observed, "[T]he term 'Hindutva' is "related more to the way of life of the people in the sub-continent. It is difficult to appreciate how in the face of [prior rulings] the term "Hindutva" or "Hinduism" per se, in the abstract, can be assumed to mean and be equated with narrow fundamentalist Hindu religious bigotry...." (p.159, para 37).

First, Rule of Law which is governance based on citizens' rights and duties, is structured in the Constitution of a nation while the enforcement mechanisms are based on procedures set out in the Constitution [e.g., Article 226 and 32 on Writs] and statutes consistent with it. The Courts provide as an independent judiciary, the interpretations of and direction to the State of the same by. In Hindu tradition, there is a highly sophisticated body of rules of interpretation and procedures prescribed in Jaimini's *Mimamsa* (in Sanskrit means "investigation") which sums up the general rules of *Nyaya*. Can we blend Mimamsa rules into the Constitution? Yes indeed. Recently, a Supreme Court judge Markandeya Katju in open court suggested the use of Mimamsa rules to fill the gaps in the traditional western Maxwell procedures in our courts.

Thus, Constitutionality consists of the *quality* of the statutes, of enforcement procedures of rights and the performance of duties, in conformity with the provisions and principles of the Constitution. This quality can be imbibed by us from the glorious Hindu texts of Mimamsa and Vedanta. In the name of modernity, defined as by our elite as anything Western, we have shown scant regard for our ancient tradition of legal argumentation. The Supreme Court on December 18, 2007 the UP State Agro Industrial Ltd case observed that the Mimamsa Rules of Interpretation (MRI) were still relevant and ought to be used in Courts alongside the traditional Maxwell Rules. Mimamsa Rules have been used by our rishis, since Jaimini wrote his Sutras, to resolve conflict betweeb various Smritis. The Supreme Court applied these Rules to classify "animal driven vehicles" in their judgment.

A Bench of Justice Markandey Katju and Justice A.K. Ganguly in its order in another case said "It is deeply regrettable that in our Courts of law, lawyers quote Maxwell and Craies but nobody refers to the MRI. Most of today's lawyers would not have even heard of its existence. Today our so-called educated people are largely ignorant about the great intellectual achievements of our ancestors and the intellectual treasury which they have bequeathed us."

The Bench said further: "the Mimansa Principles were our traditional system of interpretation of legal texts. Although originally they were created for interpreting religious texts [pertaining to the Yagya sacrifice], gradually they came to be utilised for interpreting legal texts and also for interpreting texts on philosophy, grammar, etc. i.e. they became of universal application. Thus, Shankaracharya has used the *Mimansa adhikaranas in his bhashya* on the Vedanta sutras. There were hundreds of books [all in Sanskrit] written on the subject, though only a few dozens have survived the ravages of time, but even these show how deep our ancestors went into the subject of interpretation."

The Mimansa or the Purva Mimansa Rules to be exact, were laid down by Jaimini in his *Sutras* written around 600 B.C. That they are very ancient is proved by the fact that they are referred to in many Smritis which themselves are very old. Thus, the Apastamba Sutras copiously refer to Jaimini's principles. Since these Sutras are written in very concise form it became necessary to explain them. Many commentaries were written on them, the main ones being of Sabara, who lived around Second Century A.D., and Kumarila Bhatta and Prabhakara, who lived around the Eighth Century A.D.

Before mentioning some of the Mimansa Principles it is necessary to give a short background. Classical Hindu Philosophy has six schools (shatdarshan) all of which aim at Moksha (liberation). Purva Mimansa is one of these schools, and according to it one can achieve Moksha by performing Yagya (sacrifice) in accordance with the Shastras. The Shastras consist of Shruti and Smriti, the former being superior to the latter. Shruti consists of the four Vedas, the Brahmanas, the Aranyaks and the Upanishads. Brahmanas are treatises written in prose which prescribe methods of performing various Yagyas. To every Veda one or more Brahmanas are attached. Thus, the Aitareya Brahmana is attached to the Rig Veda, the Taitareya Brahmana to the Black Yajur Veda, the Shatapatha Brahmana to the White Yajur Veda, and the Tandya Brahmana to the Sama Veda.

After Shankaracharya's historic victory over Mandana Misra, Purva Mimansa, as a philosophic system, declined in importance. Shankaracharya was a proponent of Uttar Mimansa (also known as Vedanta), according to which Moksha can be achieved by knowledge of Brahma. Shankaracharya preached that Jnanakanda (the Vedantic Path) is superior to Karmakanda (the performance of Yagya). He shifted the emphasis in the Shrutis from the Brahmanas to the Upanishads, and his view was accepted, and ever since Vedanta became the dominant school of Hindu philosophy.

However, though Purva Mimansa lost prominence to Vedanta in Philosophy, its importance remained as paramount as before in the legal sphere. It must however be clarified that the Mimansaks were not jurists. Their aim was to perform the Yagya properly, for they sincerely believed that this was the means to achieve moksha. For the conduct of Yagyas in accordance with the rules they had to devise a system of interpretation to resolve the conflicts, ambiguities, etc. in the Shrutis, which were aggravated by the archaic, pre-Panini Sanskrit employed in the Vedic texts. No doubt the principles of interpretation were initially evolved to resolve conflicts that arose in connection with the meaning of rules governing performance of the Yagya, but gradually these principles came to be accepted for interpreting legal texts also which were mixed up with religious rules in the Smritis. It was therefore natural that our great commentators like Vijnaneshwara, Jimutvahana, etc. had utilised these Mimansa principles whenever faced with any ambiguity or conflict in the various Shastras. Unfortunately, there has not been much effort to explain these principles. The advent of Anglo-Saxon Law coerced on us must have been responsible for this lack of study.

The Mimansa principles are in two respects superior to Maxwell's principles of interpretation, viz.: (1) They can be utilised not only for interpreting statutes but also judgments, whereas Maxwell's principles can only be used for interpreting statutory law, (2) They are more detailed and systematic.

The Mimansa Principles distinguish between obligatory statements and non-obligatory statements. The main obligatory rule is called a Vidhi (or a Pratishedh, if it is in negative form). Vidhis are of 4 types, (1) Utpatti Vidhi, or a substantive injunction (e.g. 'perform the agnihotra'), (2) Viniyoga Vidhi, or applicatory rules (e.g. 'with curdled milk perform the agnihotra'), (3) Prayog Vidhi, or rules of procedure, and (4) Adhikara Vidhis (rules regarding rights and personal competence). Apart from these Vidhis proper (mentioned above) there are also certain quasi Vidhis called niyamas and parishankhyas, but it is not necessary to go into details here. Vidhis are found in Brahmanas.

The main non-obligatory statement is known as an Arthavada. An Arthavada is a statement of praise or explanation. Most of the Vedas proper consist of Arthavadas as much of the Vedic hymns are in praise of some god, and do not lay down any injunction. Arthavada is like the preamble or statement of objects in a statute. An Arthavada has no legal force by itself, but it is not entirely useless since like a statement of objects or preamble it can help to clarify an ambiguous

Vidhi, or give the reason for it. Sometimes a Vidhi is also seen couched in the form of Arthavada. This situation has necessitated the need for evolving a system of interpretation. Six axioms of interpretation have therefore been developed for the interpretation of *shastras.*

Second, the Hindutva plank of restoring temples that were demolished by Islamic tyrants and mosques built on it, is constitutional thanks to the judgment in the Farooqui case. In this case [(1994) 6 SCC 361], the Constitution Bench has held that a mosque *is not an essential part of Islam and hence it can be demolished for a public purpose by a Government.* This opens the way for building a Ram temple in Ayodhya. Of course, the 1992 demolition of the Babri Masjid would have to regarded as an offence under the IPC because of a mob taking law into its own hands.

But the Babri Masjid demolition offence does not prevent a future Hindutva government from demolishing Masjids and Churches (also not an essential part of Christianity) built after demolishing Hindu temples. As the House of Lords U.K has held (1992) in the Nataraj idol case, because of *Prana prathista puja,* according to Agama Shastra, a temple is always a temple even if in disuse.

Thus for restoring the Kashi Visvanath temple or the Krishna Janmabhoomi temple, demolishing of the existing mosques by a government is constitutionally permitted. Even in the Ramjanmabhoomi temple case currently entangled on the unauthorized demolition by some people taking law into their own hands, it is an IPC offence and has no constitutional significance. Any government can even now take-over the project for public good, and build a Ram Janma bhoomi temple.

Third, Article 370 is peculiar provision. It can be deleted, without a Parliamentary amendment, by a Presidential notification, subject to the concurrence of the J&K Constituent Assembly which however has long ceased to exist. Moreover, the moral basis for it has eroded completely because the Kashmiri majority has already driven out Pandits completely altering the religious composition of the state, to preserve which the Article was incorporated. Hence, there is no fetter now to constitutionally abolish Article 370 by a notification. By way of abundant precaution the President can obtain the concurrence of the J&K Governor who legally can be treated as a proxy for the J&K Constituent Assembly.

Fourth, since the Article 44 is a Directive Principle for State Policy to have uniform *civil* code and moreover since the Muslims on ground of violation of the Shariat have not objected to a uniform *criminal* code which the Indian Penal Code is, hence it is constitutional to enforce Article 44 as not violative of Article 15, since the latter is subject to reasonable restrictions of health, morality and public order.

The question whether India should adopt a uniform civil code should be treated as a legal question because it is a mandate addressed to the 'State' by Art. 44 under Directive Principles of the Constitution. Unfortunately, in India, legal questions are politicized when it affects the "Muslim vote bank."

Article 44 of the Constitution says –

"The State shall endeavour to secure for the citizens a uniform civil code throughout the territory of India."

A controversy has however arisen as to the formation of a uniform code relating to the family or personal law of the parties relating to matters such as marriage and divorce, succession, adoption.

The framers of the Constitution clearly indicated what they meant by the word 'personal law' in Entry 5 of List III of the 7th Schedule of the same Constitution.

Entry 5 says:

"5. Marriage and divorce; infants and minors; adoption; wills; intestacy and succession; joint family and partition; all matters in respect of which parties in judicial proceedings were immediately before the commencement of this Constitution subject to their personal law."

The fathers of the Constitution had witnessed the baneful effects of a claim for separate identity of the Muslim community on the ground that their religion prescribed a separate Personal Law,—resulting in the lamentable Partition of India on the footing of the theory of 'two Nations,' founded on two religions. Hence, in the Constituent Assembly it was made clear that in a secular State personal laws relating to such matters as marriage, succession and inheritance could not depend upon religion, but must rest on the law of the land. A uniform Civil Code was accordingly necessary for achieving the unity and solidarity of the nation. [K.M. Munshi, VII C.A.D., 547-48]. Every time subsequently the question of uniform Civil Code was raised by anyone in Parliament, the Government of India opposed it on the ground that to achieve it would be to hurt Muslim 'sentiments' and that no implementation of this Directive of the fundamental law could be made so long as the Muslims themselves would not come forward to ask for it. [see Prime Minister Rao [Statesman, 1-6-1995; 28-7-1995], and also at his Independence Day Speech at Red Fort on 15-8-1995; Law Minister, Bharadwaj [Jugantar, 12-12-1993; Statesman, 22-7-1995]; Gadgil, Secretary General of Congress (I) Party [Vartaman, 21-4-1995]; Dinesh

Goswami, Law Minister [U.N.I., 22-12-1989]. Nevertheless, the Supreme Court has recommended, more than once, to take early steps towards the formation of a uniform Civil Code [Mudgal v. Union of India (1995) 3 S.C.C. 635 — Kuldip Singh & Sahai JJ. (10th May, 1995).

That the Shariat is not infallible or immutable is evidenced by the patent fact that it has been discarded on modified in many respects by various Muslim States. And this has been achieved in an orthodox Muslim State such as Tunisia, through the process of liberal or progressive interpretation of the scriptures.

Advocates of immutability should be silenced by the following observations of a Muslim Judge of Pakistan, Huq, J., of the Lahore High Court –

"it would not be correct to lay it down as a positive rule of law that the present-day Courts in this country should have no power or authority to interpret the Quran in a way different from that adopted by the earlier Jurists and Imams. The adoption of such a view is likely to endanger the dynamic and universal character of the religion and laws of Quran."

The ground of immutability of the Shariat was in fact raised by some Muslim members in the Constituent Assembly of India but was rejected on the opposition from Dr. Ambedkar. It would be an eyeopener to many today to recount what Ambedkar said [VII C.A.D. 55] in this context.

"... up to 1935 the North-West Frontier Province was not subject to Shariat Law; it followed the Hindu Law in the matter of succession and in other matters, so much so that it was in 1939 that the Central Legislature had to come into the field and to abrogate the application of the Hindu Law to Muslims of North-West Frontier Province and to apply Shariat Law to them ... apart from North-West Frontier Province, up till 1937 in the rest of India, in various parts, such as the United Provinces, the Central Provinces and Bombay, the Muslims to a large extent were governed by the Hindu Law in the matter of succession ... that in North-Malabar the Marumakkathayam law applied to all—not only to Hindus but also to Muslims." [op.cit]

Even in India the Koranic laws of crimes and evidence have been supplanted as early as the 19th century by enacting the Penal Code and the Evidence Act, e.g., by saving the Muslims from the following mediaeval atrocities which are still prevalent in Muslim countries like Pakistan and Bangladesh.

(a) Chopping off the hands of a criminal as a punishment for theft, or stoning to death as a punishment for adultery.

(b) Adultery and apostasy being punishable by death.

(c) Where the witnesses are women, their value as against the evidence of men is in the ratio of 2:1.

The entire law of criminal procedure has been replaced in India by statute. The Indians laws of crimes and evidence make no distinction between Muslims and non-Muslims. The Judges in a Muslim dispute need not be Muslims.

In this context, one critic has pointed out that in Goa, from the days of Portuguese rule, the people have been governed by a uniform civil code, but for the matter of that, Goanese Muslims have not lost their identity or culture.

If it is contended that personal law, founded on religion, has any special status, the answer is that it is the British Parliament which made the English Crown the head of the Church and altered the law of royal succession; and an Indian Parliament superseded the Hindu law of marriage and succession, in the teeth of opposition from an enlightened section of Hindus. It was opposed by Dr. Rajendra Prasad himself on the grounds that Art.44, being applicable to all persons in the territory of India, should not be imposed on the Hindus alone and that the Government who sponsored the Hindu Code Bill to replace the personal law of the Hindus had no mandate from the Electorate in this behalf.

Above all, the Muslims who remained in India after the Partition did so with the full knowledge that divided India was going to adopt a Parliamentary system of democracy and not any Muslim system of the Middle Ages where Shariat would be the supreme law of the land. They should also have known that a personal law founded on the religion of different communities was incompatible with the very concept of a 'Secular' State which divided India was going to be.

Factually also, the assumption of the Government of India that the entire Muslim community is opposed to the implementation of Art.44 is not correct. The Shah Bano case demonstrated that it was only a section of the Sunni sect amongst the Muslims which was vehemently opposed to the judgment.

The Supreme Court can no more wash its hands off Art. 44 on the ground that it is a Directive Principle which is not directly enforceable. Jordan v. Chopra (1985) 3 S.C.C 62 Besides, some Supreme Court Judges had expressed their views to the same effect out of Court: Gajendragadkar, C.J., and Chairman, Law Commission, in his book—Secularism and the Constitution of India (1971), p. 126; Shelat, J., Secularism, Principles and Application (1972); Hegde, J., in the Law Institute, in January, 1972; Tulzapurkar, J., —article in A.I.R. 1987 Jours. 17; Beg. C.J., in his Motilal Nehru Lecture on 'Impact of Secularism on Life and Law.' Prior to Kuldip Singh, J., in numerous cases, the

Supreme Court has remedied the inaction of the Government in other clauses of Directive Principles to implement various Directives, in Arts. 38, 39, 39A, 41, 42, 43, by issuing 'directions' which are mentioned in Art. 32(2) as legitimate instruments in the hands of the Court.

Even in the matter of Art. 44, previous Benches of the Supreme Court had commented upon the inaction of the Government and the need for an early implementation of the Article –

(a) A unanimous Constitution Bench in the Shah Bano case (para. 32).

(b) A Division Bench, speaking through Chinnappa Reddy, J., in Jordan's case.

That the Shariat on personal law is not sacrosanct will appear from the following examples of Muslim majority countries which have superseded or modified polygamy.

Turkey: The Court can declare a second marriage as invalid on the ground that a spouse is living at the time of the second marriage [Turkish Civil Code, Art. 74].

Pakistan: A person cannot contract a second marriage without the permission of the Arbitration Council; and a wife can obtain divorce on the ground that the husband has married another wife.

Iran: A person cannot remarry without permission of the Court.

Egypt, Jordan, Morocco, Syria: Similar restrictions on bigamy as in Iran and Pakistan have been imposed in Egypt, Jordan, Morocco and Syria.

Tunisia: Bigamy is totally prohibited by the Tunisia Law of personal Status (s. 18).

Registration of all marriages, including those contracted in conformity with Shariat formalities, has been made compulsory in Iran, Algeria, Indonesia, Malaysia.

There is no reason why such law cannot be adopted in India.

Fifth, the call for Hindutva has been held by the Supreme Court in Manohar Joshi [1996] case to be within the Constitutional requirements of free speech. Hence, time has arrived for us to openly declare India as an ancient Hindu civilization, which is the only way we can perform the Fundamental Duty under Article 51-A(f), and boldly up revere our sacred symbols. For example, the total ban on cow slaughter in Article 48 has been held by a 1958 Constitution Bench to possess constitutionality in the sense that the total ban is held to be a reasonable restriction on fundamental rights of all Indians.

Sixth, at present the Government has been taking over Hindu temples its resources and land and using it for all kinds of non-religious purposes under the states enacted Hindu Religious Institutions and Charitable Endowment Acts on the pretext of maladministration of the temple properties. Under Article 31A of the Constitution such a take-over cannot be permanent. If maladministration charge is true, then the Government should rectify it within a reasonable period such as three years, and then hand it back. At present State governments have taken over tens of thousands of temples for decades. Time is now to get them released.

These six constitutionally valid pillars are what Hindutva is, and it is significant that Hindutva goals can be achieved within the present Constitution.

DHARMA NIRPEKSHTA AND SARVA PANTHA SAMA BHAAVA

Throughout ancient Indian history, Hindu kingdoms, never required any 'subject' to be of Hindu religion in order to be regarded a first class citizen. Only in Asoka's reign and Islamic rule, India was a theocracy. Hindu is naturally 'Secular.' But secularism is a much-bandied-about subject nowadays. Unfortunately, those political parties who have been swearing by it all these years have failed to persuade the masses that secularism is good for country.

In fact, secularism as defined and propagated today has lost its relevance. The concept as understood by the masses of India stands thoroughly discredited. Hence the question is whether we should redefine secularism in keeping our civilization tradition to make it acceptable to the masses or capitulate to the rising fundamentalism in the country with dire consequences for national integrity and security.

When Rev. Martin Luther had defined secularism in Europe, it simply meant that the power of the state would be exercised independently of the directions of the Church. Thus, a secular government would act to safeguard the nation-state, even if such action was without Church sanction. Later, Marx calling religion the 'opium of the masses' defined secularism to completely eschew religion.

In India, Jawaharlal Nehru and his followers subscribed to the later Marxist redefinition of the concept in which even in public functions, cultural symbolism such as lighting a lamp to inaugurate a conference or breaking a coconut to launch a project was regarded as against secularism. This orthodoxy induced a reaction in the Indian masses. Nehru failed to define what historical roots ought to be a part of the modem Indian, and what was to be rejected. In the name of 'scientific temper,' he rejected most of our past as 'obscurantism.' His orthodox secularism sought to alienate the Indian from his hoary past. Since nearly 85 percent of Indians are pan-Hindu in beliefs, and Hindu religion from its inception has been without a 'Church,' 'Pope' or 'Book' (in contradistinction to Christianity), therefore neither Martin Luther nor Marx made any sense to the Indian masses. Since there was little political challenge to Nehru after the untimely death of Gandhiji and Patel, the Marxian secularism concept superficially prevailed till Nehru's demise in 1964. The masses therefore humoured Nehru without accepting his concept of secularism. A Conceptual void however remained to be filled.

But Congress Party continued thereafter to fail to provide a political concept of secularism by which an Indian citizen could comprehend how he should bond "secularly" with another citizen of a different religion or language, or region and feel equally Indian. The Hindu instinctively could not accept the idea that India was what the British had put together, and that the country was just an area incorporated by the imperialists. Such a ridiculous idea, fostered quixotically by Jawaharlal Nehru University historians, found just no takers amongst the Indian people. The void remained thus, but the yearning in the masses to be "Indian" grew over the years with growth of mass media. This void had therefore to be filled and the yearning of national identity required to be articulated for the masses.

The legal perspective on Indian secularism has been brilliantly analysed by Supreme Justice Aftab Alam [in (2009) 10SCC J-60]. While he disapproves of the trends in, and import of the various Supreme Court decisions since 1994, however I welcome them. But I salute his research, which I have used in this Chapter *in fact to prove my point* viz., the Indian

Constitution as increasingly interpreted by the Supreme Court is basically becoming 'Hindutva-friendly.'

The Constitution of India recognises twenty-two languages as Indian languages. Indians speaking the same language may belong to different religions. India is home to eight major religions of the world. Conversely, Indians belonging to the same religious group may come from different parts of the national geography and may speak different languages, dress differently, eat different kinds of food in entirely different manners and may have completely different social and economic concerns. In India, religion, a democratic State, and secularism overlap and combine to display a highly interesting and unique society.

India has survived while others with the same concerns have balkanized. But the important fact is that the liberality implicit in the Indian system is owed to the Hindu ethos of our civilization. I elaborate with some specific examples! There are six different ways, sanctioned by law, in which an Indian, depending on his or her religion, can get married. The one mode of solemnisation of marriage that requires formal registration which applies to all Indians irrespective of religion *finds favour with very few.*

As Justice Aftap Alam points out: "The vast body of law dealing with property rights treats two Indians differently, again depending upon their religion. On my death the devolution of my estate upon my heirs will take place in a way completely different than in case of my Hindu friends."

Among Hindus the concept of joint family is quite inseparable from the Hindu way of life. The institution of Hindu Undivided Family or joint family is woven into a number of laws with the result that those laws affect different people quite differently.

For every Muslim going for Haj, the Government of India spends from the taxpayers' money, a substantial amount as airfare subsidy if the pilgrims fly Air India. In the Government of India budget for the year 2009-2010 a sum of Rs. 632 crores (approx.77.53 million pounds) is allocated as Haj subsidy. It is likely to be Rs. 850 crores in 2010-11.

But, Kumbh Mela of Hindus or the Fair of the divine nectar pot, takes place four times every twelve years when millions of Hindu pilgrims congregate to take the holy dip in the river on a single day. In 2010 in Haridwar where the Ganges comes down into the plain the most recent Fair has taken place. The State of Uttarakhand would spend an estimated amount of Rs.500 crores (approx. 62.53 million pounds) for organising the mela.

Besides the Kumbh there would be at least a dozen purely religious festivals where direct government spending would run into thousands of crores of rupees. But unlike for Muslims, no Hindu is paid any subsidy by the State for travel to the Kumbh and for stay there.

The Indian Constitution does not have any provision, unlike the First Amendment of the United States Constitution, proscribing the making of any law respecting an establishment of religion. *It instead recognises religion as a source of law.* With a view to protect minority rights, it confers affirmative social and cultural rights on religious groups. It guarantees the fundamental freedom of religion but enables the State, to regulate religious practices on certain limited grounds of morality, health and public order.

Thus, under the Indian Constitution, secularism of the State involves a plural establishment of religion with the State but maintaining of *equidistance* from all religions. The Court is called upon, in a variety of ways, to oversee and regulate the *distance* that the State ought to keep from religious establishments and the nature of State intervention permissible in religious affairs. *In that sense it would be more appropriate to designate India as a spiritual state rather than a secular state*. But confusion prevails today in the judiciary on how far to stretch secularism and how cognizant the law should be of the Hindu ethos of the nation.

For instance, keeping a beard by a Muslim student invoked Article 25 of the Constitution that gives to every person (in this case the Muslim student) the freedom of conscience and free profession and practice of religion. A Christian missionary-run school defended its rules not to permit it students with beards and expelled the Muslim student on the basis of Article 30 of the Constitution that gives to all minorities (in this case the Christian) the right to establish and administer educational institutions. The expulsion was challenged unsuccessfully before the High Court and the matter finally came to the Supreme Court. On 30-3-2009 the petition was dismissed *in limine* but in course of the brief hearing, one of the judges made certain observations that were widely reported in the media. The Judge had said: "We don't want to have Talibans in the country. Tomorrow a girl student may come and say that she wants to wear a burqa, can we allow it?" [Times of India, March 31, 2009] He further said: "We should strike a balance between rights and personal beliefs. We cannot overstretch secularism." Hence, the Judge added: "You can join some other institution if you do not want to observe the rules. But you can't ask the school to change the rules for you."

The remarks created an uproar among the Muslims against the remarks calling the beard and the burqa as the mark of the Taliban. Then, on 6-7-2009, on a review petition, the same

Bench recalled its order dismissing the petition and requested the Chief Justice to have the case placed before some other Bench. On 11-9-2009 the case came up before another Bench. *And this time the response of the Court was completely different*: "How on earth could a school disentitle a student from pursuing studies just because he has kept a beard? Then there will be no end to such prima facie ridiculous rules."

This exemplifies the difficulties faced by the Court in dealing with two 'competing' constitutional rights in Articles 25 and 30. The first Bench obviously gave precedence to the group right guaranteed by the Constitution (Article 30) to a religious minority, in this case the Christian management of the school. The second Bench, on the other hand, deemed fit, in the context of the case, to uphold the right of the individual (Article 25), the Muslim boy. This deep dilemma, as Justice Alam points out seems to run through the decisions of the Supreme Court on the issue of cultural and educational rights guaranteed by the Constitution to the religious minorities.

In 1957, the Communist Government of Kerala enacted a law bringing the school education in the State under its extensive control. A number of Christian organizations and some Muslim groups threatened to create a political crisis.

The President of India to whom the Bill had come for his assent therefore made a reference to the Supreme Court on the constitutional validity of the Bill. A Constitution Bench of seven Judges, headed by Chief Justice S.R. Das, heard the matter and held [AIR 1958 SC 956] that Article 30 was a *stand-alone* Article and the right guaranteed to the minorities under it was not controlled either by Article 29 or any other Article in the chapter of fundamental rights, or even Article 45 in the chapter of Directive Principles relating to education to children below the age of six years. Speaking for the Court S.R. Das, C.J. said:

> "... So long as the Constitution stands as it is and is not altered, it is, we conceive, the duty of this Court to uphold the fundamental rights and thereby honour our sacred obligation to the minority communities who are our own" (p.986).

The decision in *Kerala Education Bill, 1957,* however, was not unanimous. There was at least one dissenting voice (of Justice T. L. Venkatarama Aiyar). He took the view that Article 30 was primarily intended to protect educational institutions established for the conservation and promotion of the *culture, language or religion* of a minority group and thus created a purely negative obligation on the State and prevented it from interfering with minorities living their own cultural life as regards religion or language. Justice Aiyar observed:

> "... Now, to compel the State to recognise those institutions would conflict with the fundamental concept on which the Constitution is framed *that the State should be secular in character*." (p.989)

The two views directly opposing each other and both relying upon the principles of secularism that were manifested in *Kerala Education Bill* appear to run through the decisions of the Supreme Court on all *aspects of* secularism. But with the sole exception in *S. Azeez Basha* v. *Union of India (Aligarh Muslim University case* [AIR 1968 SC 662]) the majority decision in *Kerala Education Bill* was relied upon to expand the scope of the right under Article 30, and five years later in *Sidhrajbhai Sabbai*

v. *State of Gujarat* (AIR 1963 SC 540) a six-Judge constitutional Bench went on to hold:

> "The right [under] Article 30(1) is a fundamental right declared in terms absolute. Unlike the fundamental freedoms guaranteed by Article 19 *it is not subject to reasonable restrictions.*" (p.547).

Soon secularism came to be regarded as not only a fundamental right but a part of the basic structure of the Constitution. In the Bommai case [(1994)3 SCC 1] seven out of the nine Judges constituting the Bench reiterated the view that secularism was the basic feature of the Constitution and in case a State Government acted contrary to the constitutional mandate of secularism or, worse still, directly or indirectly, subverted the secular principles, *that_would tantamount to failure of the constitutional machinery and the State Government would make itself liable to dismissal under Article 356* (para 434).

But soon enough, the Court started to see the interplay between the community based rights and individual rights in a new light. In *Stephen's College,* a Delhi Christian minority college the Court felt the need to strike a balance between an individual's right based on merits and the right of minorities to set up and administer educational institutions of their choice and directed that *St. Stephen's College* could have no more than fifty per cent seats reserved for Christian students. Thus, the right under Article 30 was for the first time subject to Article 29 reversing the earlier ominous trend for the better. Article 29 states:

Protection of interests of minorities.—(1) Any section of the citizens residing in the territory of India or any part thereof having a distinct language, script or culture of its own shall have the right to conserve the same.

As Justice Alam infers, by 2005, this reversing trend was fortified by several decisions till in the end of Article 30 all but lost its independent identity. The position that emerges from these decisions may be summarised thus:

- The right to set up educational institutions and impart any kind of education at any level is available to every Indian citizen under Article 19(1)(g) of the Constitution as the right "to carry on any occupation, trade or business."
- Article 30 does not give to the religious minorities any additional or separate right. *The religious minority has no special right that the majority does not have under the Constitution.*
- Articles 29 and 30 do not confer any rights but afford certain protections to the minorities. The two articles can be better understood as a protection and/or a privilege of the minority rather than an abstract right. (View of Venkatarama, J. in minority of 1:6 in *Kerala Education Bill,* was thus resurrected!)
- The right under Article 30 is not absolute. It is subject to Article 29(2) and other laws. *It can be restricted in public interest and national interest.*

The Supreme Court's perception of secularism, also underwent change since the Bommai case of 1994 through a catena of judgments since 1995.

In 2002 a public interest litigation [(2002) 7 SCC 368] was filed questioning the curriculum for school education framed by the National Council for Educational Research and Training on the ground that it was heavily loaded with religion and the contents of the Vedas. It was contended that the inclusion of religion, Sanskrit, Vedic Mathematics, Vedic Astrology, etc. in the courses of study for the schools was contrary to secular principles.

Justice Dharmadhikari one of the members of the three-Judge Bench wrote a separate, though concurring judgment in which he discussed in some detail about the true nature of secularism. He observed that the doctrine of the State neutrality towards all religions was a narrow concept of secularism. He further observed that the policy of complete neutrality towards and apathy for all kinds of religious teachings in institutions of the State had not done any good to the country. *The real meaning of secularism is 'sarva dharma samabhav'* meaning equal treatment and respect for all religions, but, we misunderstood the meaning of secularism as negation of all religions." (page 406-407)

In 2005, an organisation representing a section of the Jain community came to the Court seeking a direction to the Central Government to notify "Jains" as a minority community. The Court not only firmly rejected the prayer but also expressed its strong disapproval of the very concept of "minority." Calling it a baggage from India's history, the Court noted *(Bal Patil case, SCC* p. 701, para 25): "Muslims constituted the largest religious minority because the Mughal period of rule was the longest followed by the British Rule during which many Indians had adopted Muslim and Christian religions." It further observed that the concept of "minorities" was the result of the British policy of divide and rule that first led to the formation of separate electorates and reservations of seats on the basis of population of Hindus and Muslims and finally led to the partition of India and formation of a separate Muslim State of Pakistan. The Court pointed out that India was a democratic republic which had adopted the right to equality as its fundamental creed and hence, the constitutional ideal should be the elimination of "minority" and "majority" and the so-called forward and backward classes.

All that remains now is further decisions of the Supreme Court to restrict the meaning of minorities to cover *only ethnic minorities whose DNA is different from majority of Indians*. That would mean only a few tribes of extreme Northeast and Onge tribes in Andamans, but not Muslims and Christians who are not recent converts. Affirmative action of the State however can be extended only to those minorities which have suffered from imposed disabilities, and not those minorities which have been ruling classes. The term 'Secularism' should also be replaced in the Constitution by the alternative more appropriate phrase "spiritual state based on 'Sarva Pantha Sama Bhava.'

The Supreme Court has also tried to regulate the efforts of the State to control religious affairs in the context of Article 26 of the Constitution. Article 26 gives to every religious denomination or any section thereof the freedom to manage its religious affairs, *subject, however to considerations of public order, morality and health*. The extent of the right in evolved from the *essential practices test* according to which immunity from State intervention was available to only such practices that were integral to the faith and not to other practices pertaining to economic and commercial matters though associated with religion [(1954) 1 SCR 1005].

The Court thus preferred to lay down the test, rather than subjecting the law to the test of public order, morality and health (to which Articles 25 and 26 rights are subject). Thus, instead of denying constitutional protection on the ground that a certain practice violated public order, morality or health, the Court preferred simply to hold that a certain practice was not an essential part of a particular religion. The Court also assumed to itself the right to decide whether or not a certain practice was essential to a religion, of course with reference to authoritative sources and texts relating to that religion.

When the Swaminarayana sect took the plea that they did not belong to the Hindu religion and hence their temples were not covered by the Act prohibiting Hindu temples from refusing entry to Harijans, the Court referred to several texts on Hinduism and Indology and concluded that the Swaminarayana sect was indeed a part the Hindu religion, and their temples were fully covered by the provisions of the Act.

In giving itself the power to judge what was an essential practice of a religion—the Court could now hold that those were essential practices *could not avail of the protection of Article 25*. This had enabled the Court to adopt an extremely interventionist approach—even resorting to Scriptural Interpretation. I welcome this.

In Shah Bano case [(1985)2 SCC 556] the statutory provisions of maintenance of divorced wives were held to be applicable to Muslims, in view of the Muslim Personal Law (Shariat) Application Act, 1937. The Court held that there was nothing in the Muslim Personal Law that conflicted with the statutory provisions for maintenance. The decision created resentment against the Court amongst Muslim clerics for arrogating to itself the right and the authority to interpret the Quran, forgetting that the Court had consistently resorted to scriptural interpretation while applying the essential practices test to the Hindu religion.

For political considerations however the Central Government abjectly surrendered and had Parliament pass a legislation. The new Act was challenged in *Danial Latifi case* [(2001)7 SCC 740] *as* violative of the constitutional right of the Muslim woman to obtain statutory maintenance beyond the *iddat* period, which had been upheld in *Shah Bano.* The Court, now while upholding the constitutional validity of the Act, was paradoxically also able to preserve all the rights given to a Muslim divorcee woman in *Shah Bano case,* observing that "it may look ironical that the enactment intended to reverse the decision in *Shah Bano case,* actually codifies the very rationale contained therein."

What, however, is of great significance is that in *Danial Latifi* case the Court reached the same reformist conclusion as in *Shah Bano* but through a different, and more acceptable, route. The Court instead had subjected the Act to the test of Articles 14, 15 and 21 of the Constitution. It effectively held that the Act would be unconstitutional if interpreted to give Muslim women less than other women by way of maintenance.

Thus, if this trend of decisions of the Supreme Court continues, then, it is a matter of time before the issue of minority rights will be addressed afresh, having regard to the concerns and in light of the experience of the past sixty years. By this trend I would hazard a guess: *Hindutva will sooner or later in the future become the basis of Indian jurispudence.*

Another issue is of religious conversions carried out by proselytizing religions of Islam and Christianity.

In Rev. Satya Ranjan Majhi and Anr v. State of Orissa and Ors. [AIR 2003 Ori 163]:

As we have noticed, the Supreme Court has clearly held that the right to convert another person to one's own religion was not covered by Article 25(1) of the Constitution of India and there was no fundamental right in any one to convert another person to one's own religion."

Mahatma Gandhi foresaw this possibility. Writing in *Harijan* (before May 11, 1935) he opined: "If I had the power and could legislate, I should stop all proselytizing. In Hindu households the advent of the missionary has meant the disruption of the family coming in the wake of change of dress, manners, language, food and drink."

In *Harijan* (April 3, 1937) he again wrote: "When the missionary of another religion goes to them, he goes like a vendor of goods. He has no special spiritual merit that will distinguish him from those to whom he goes. He does however possess material goods which he promises to those who will come to his fold."

The revered Swami Dayananda Sarasvati, National Convenor, Hindu Dharma Acharya Sabha and pioneer in inter-faith dialogue, wrote in 1999 to the Pope of Vatican that to support conversion of religious faith for whatever reason was a form of violence.

The Constituent Assembly decided the word "propagate" in Art. 25(1) be introduced in the Constitution indeed to enable religious conversion of persons to other religions.

But it was never the case in the Assembly debates that anyone be allowed to convert to another religion through inducements or force or fraud.

Moreover, the Constituent Assembly members were unanimous that such conversion would be void, as if it had never happened, if it was made through force, fraud and inducement.

The notable speeches in the Constituent Assembly against forcible conversion were made by K.M. Munshi, F.R. Anthony, R.P. Thakur, J.J. Nichols Roy, Purushottamdas Tandon, Algu Rai Shastri, Ananthasayanam Ayyangar, Hussain Imam, K. Santhanam. See Sardar Vallabhbhai Patel.

In fact two members Tajamul Husain and K. M. Munshi wanted even the word "propagate" deleted from Article 25. The intention of our Freedom Movement leaders in the Constituent Assembly was clear and against unfettered right to convert anybody as can be seen by the suggested amendments that were negative.

Hence, it cannot be an argument that a law or section(s) of such a law, which makes coercive and corrupt methods of conversion as criminal offences, is ultra vires Article 25 or any other fundamental rights enshrined in the Constitution.

This has been affirmed by a Constitutional Bench of the Supreme Court in the Rev. Stanislaus vs State of Madhya Pradesh [AIR 1977 SC 908 or (1977) 1 SCC 677, paras. 15A, 17 to 24, p. 911-12] in wherein it was held that "... there can therefore, be no such thing as a fundamental right to convert any person to one's own religion." [para 20].

In fact, the Hon'ble Bench made it explicit that the scope of Article 25 of the Constitution did not include the protection for "the right to convert another person to one's own religion but to transmit or spread one's religion by an exposition of its tenets...." [para 18].

The Hon'ble Apex Court in the said Stanislaus case went on to observe that "it cannot be predicated that freedom of religion can have no bearing whatever on the maintenance of public order or that a law creating an offence relating to religion cannot under any circumstances be said to have been enacted in the interest of public order" [para 24].

Therefore, the Hon'ble Constitutional Bench of the Apex Court held that Acts (by inference such laws as HPFRA) fall within the purview of Entry II of the Seventh Schedule of the Constitution "as they are meant to avoid disturbances to the public order by prohibiting conversion from one religion to another in a manner reprehensible to the conscience of the community" [*Ibid*].

This ruling has since been re-affirmed in recent judgments of the Hon'ble Supreme Court. In Rabindra Kumar Pal @ Dara Singh v. Republic of India [Criminal Appeal No. 1366 of 2005 judgment dated January 25, 2011] the Court held: (para 97) "It is undisputed that there is no justification for interfering in someone's belief by way of 'use of force,' provocation, conversion, incitement or upon a flawed premise that one religion is better than the other."

However, the reported judgment in (2011) 2 SCC 490 reads: (para 97) "There is no justification for interfering in someone's religious belief by any means." The reported judgment refers to a clarificatory Order dated 25-1-2011 which amended para 97.

Annexure A-1

Chronology of Major Events Related to Ayodhya

1528	Mosque built in Ayodhya, which Hindus believe to be the birthplace of Shri Ram, by Mir Baqi, a noble in Emperor Babur's court.
1855	Records of a battle in Ayodhya.
1859	British administration erects a fence to separate places of worship, allowing the inner court to be used by Muslims and the outer court by Hindus.
1885	Suit filed praying for permission to erect a temple on outer court close to mosque; the suit is denied.
1934	Communal riots occur over the use of the disputed structure.
23 December 1949	Ram Lalla idols are installed in the RJM/BM*. A lock is put on the structure by orders of the magistrate under Section 145 Cr. PC.
January 1950	Two title suits are filed by Gopal Singh Visharad and Paramhans Ramachandra. Interim injunction orders are passed therein by the Civil Judge to allow pooja and not to remove idols.

*Ramjanambhoomi – Babri Masjid

3 March 1951	Civil Judge confirms interim injunction order.
26 April 1955	High Court confirms interim injunction order dated 3 March 1951.
1959	Title suit filed by Nirmohi Akhara.
1961	Title suit filed by Sunni Central Waqf Board.
1984	Vishwa Hindu Parishad begins campaign to build a Ram temple at Ayodhya.
1 February 1986	Order passed by District Judge for opening locks of the RJB-BM and allowing pooja by devotees.
February 1986	Prominent Muslim leaders decide to form Babri Masjid Action Committee.
July 1988-November 1989	Discussions held by Buta Singh, Union Home Minister, with various parties relating to RKB-BM issue.
1989	Title suit filed by D.N. Agarwal. Original title suis transferred to High Court and consolidated for being taken up together.
14 August 1989	Order passed by High Court for maintenance of status quo of disputed property.
October-November 1989	Pujan shilas (bricks) brought from all over the country to Ayodhya.
9 November 1989	Shilanyas of the proposed Ram temple performed at a site agreed between various sides as being undisputed.
February 1990	Kar seva at RJB-BM.
July-October 1990	Negotiations during the government of V.P. Singh.
September-October	Advani's rath yatra.

1990

19 October 1990	The Ramjanamabhoomi-Babri Masjid (Acquisition of Area) Ordinance, 1990 promulgated to aquifer the disputed shrine and its adjoining area.
23 October 1990	The Ramjanamaboomi-Babri Masjid (Acquisition of Area) Withdrawal Ordinance 1990 promulgaed to cancel the earlier Ordinance.
30 October 1990	Kar seva at RJB-BM. Some devotees climb the domes of RJB-BM, damage them and hoist saffron flags. Some damage also done to compound walls of RJB-BM. The situation is brought under control quickly by the Central and State Governments, led by V.P. Singh and Mulayam Singh Yadav respectively.
2 November 1990	Use of force at Ayodhya leads to death of some people. Riots in may parts of the country follow.
9 December 1990	Attempt to blow up shrine.
December 1990-February 1991	Negotiations during the government of Chandra Shekhar.
June 1991	General elections. BJP government formed in UP. Congress government headed by P. V. Narasimha Rao comes to power at the Centre.
7, 10 October 1991	Notifications for land acquisition issued by Government of UP. This is followed by demolition of certain structures on acquired land.
25 October 1991	High Court passes order in writ petitions, inter alia, allowing Government of UP to

	take possession of acquired land but prohibiting permanent construction.
31 October 1991	Some people attack the structure and cause some damage to its walls.
2 November 1991	Meeting of National Integration Council. CM's assurances. Unanimous resolution passed.
15 November 1991	Supreme Court passes order noting CM's assurances to NIC and High Court's order of 25 October 1991 and directing compliance with these.
December 1991 Onwards	Construction of boundary wall (Ram Diwar) started in Ayodhya.
February 1991	Construction of boundary wall (Ram Diwar) started in Ayodhya.
March 1991	42.09 acres of land acquired in 1988 and 1989 handed over by UP Government to RJB Nyas and for Ram Katha Park.
March-May 1992	All other structures on acquired land demolished.
May 1991	Extensive digging and leveling operations. (High Court refuses to stay these operations).
9 July 1992	Construction of concrete platform commenced.
15 July 1992	High Court prohibits undertaking or continuing construction activity.
July 1992	Contempt petitions filed in Supreme Court. (Some petitions had been filed earlier also).
23 July 1992	Supreme Court prohibits construction activity of any kind. P.V. Narasimha Raos' meeting with religious leaders.
26 July 1992	Construction activity stops.

27 July 1992	P.V. Narasimha Rao's statement in Parliament.
August-September 1992	Ayodhya Cell set up in PMO. P.V. Narasimha Raos' meeting with various leaders.
October 1992	Two meetings between VHP and BMAC in resumed negotiations.
23 October 1992	Meeting for study of archaeological material between VHP and BMAC nominees.
30 and 31 October 1992	Dharam Sansad/KMDM meetings. Announcement made for resumption of kar seva on 6 Decembeer 1992.
8 November 1992	Third and last meeting between VHP and BMAC.
23 November 1992	NIC meeting boycotted by BJP. Unanimous resolution passed. Government of India makes submissions before Supreme Court following is directive on 20 November 1992.
24 November 1992	CPMF's stationed at places near Ayodhya by Central Government.
26 November 1992	Supreme Court passes order regarding Ayodhya.
27, 28 November 1992	Affidavits/assurances given by government of UP. Supreme Court passes order classifying that kar seva would be symbolic and not entail construction. Court appoints Observer.
6 December 1992	Date of kar seva. RJB-BM attacked and demolished by kar sevaks. Idols removed and reinstalled. A wall and shed erected on 6 and 7 December. President's Rule imposed in UP. UP Assembly dissolved.
Night of 7-8 December 1992	CPMFs take control of RJB-BM area.

December 1992	BJP brings no-confidence motion against P.V. Narasimha Rao's government in Parliament; the motion is defeated.
27 December 1992	Central Government decides to take over RJB-BM site.
7 January 1993	Acquisition of Certain Area at Ayodhya Ordinance issued. Core question of dispute referred to Supreme Court by President of India.
January 1993	Bomb blasts, thought to be orchestrated in retaliation to the Babri Masjid demolition, rock Mumbai; thousands die in the resultant communal riots.
24 December 1994	Supreme Court passes judgment on Ayodhya incident, holds Kalyan Singh's government responsible.
1998	BJP comes to power at the Centre.
2002	BJP withdraws from its commitment to built a Ram temple at Ayodhya. VHP sets deadline of 15 March to begin construction of temple. Kar sevaks from across the country converge on Ayodhya. Compartment of Sabarmati Express carrying kar sevaks burns down in Godhra, Gujarat, killing a number of people. Thousands die in communal riots in Gujarat following the incident. Meanwhile, three High Court judges begin hearings to determine who owns the disputed site.
2003	Archaeological Survey of India begins a court-ordered survey to find out whether a temple to Ram existed on the disputed site. The survey says there is evidence of a temple beneath the mosque; Muslims dispute the findings. A court rules that seven Hindu

	leaders should stand trial for inciting the destruction of the Babri Masjid in 1992.
2004	Congress government comes to power at the Centre after six years of BJP rule. Leader of the Opposition L.K. Advani says his party has an unwavering commitment to building a Ram temple at Ayodhya.
5 July 2005	Six heavily-armed terrorists make an attempt to storm the high-security makeshift Ram temple at Ayodhya. The attack is thwarted and all terrorists killed by security forces.
2010	Lucknow Bench of Allahabad High Court gives its judgement. The Bench gave separate judgements for each of the three judges. But the Bench concurred that Lord Rama was the owner of one of the dones and place as his birth place.
2011	All parties appeal against the judgement in SLPs to the Supreme Court.

Annexure A-2

Map of Acquired Area (67 acres) Ram Janambhoomi, Ayodhya

under Acquisition of Certain Area Act No. 33 of 1993

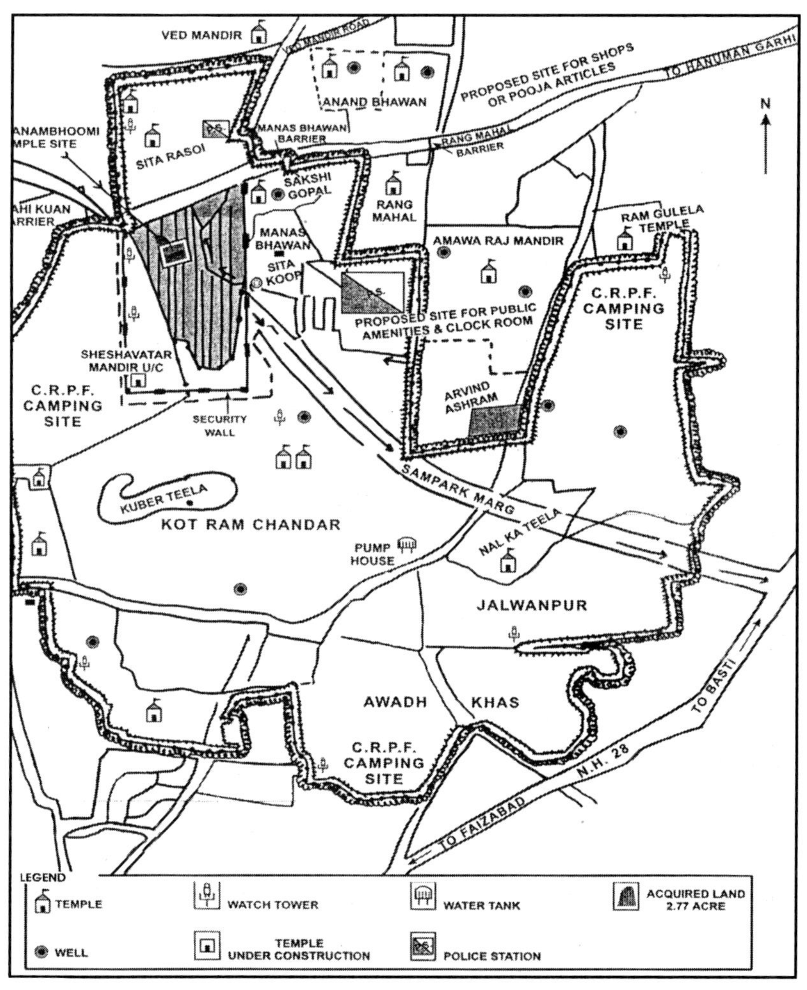

Annexure A-3

Solicitor General's Affidavit Para 105

5. And whereas notwithstanding the vesting of the aforesaid area in the Central Government under the said Ordinance the Central Government proposes to settle the said dispute after obtaining the opinion of the Supreme Court of India and in terms of the said opinion;

6. And whereas in view of what has been hereinbefore stated it appears to me that the question hereinafter set out has arisen and is of such a nature and of such public importance that it is expedient to obtain the opinion of the Supreme Court of India thereon;

7. Now, therefore, in exercise of the powers conferred upon me by clause (1) of Article 143 of the Constitution of India, I, Shanker Dayal Sharma, President of India, hereby refer the following question to the Supreme Court of India for consideration and opinion thereon, namely,

Whether a Hindu temple or any Hindu religious structure existed prior to the construction of the Ram Janma Bhumi-Babri Masjid (including the premises of the inner and outer courtyards of such structure) in the area on which the structure stood?"

105. It will be seen that the fifth recital of the Reference states that "the Central Government proposes to settle te said dispute after obtaining the opinion of the Supreme Court of India and in terms of the said opinion." The learned Solicitor General, appearing for the Central Government, submitted that this meant that the Central Government "was committed to bring about a settlement in the light of the Supreme Court opinion and consistent therewith. However, at this stage it cannot be predicated as to the precise manner in which progress towards a solution could be made," If, he submitted orally, no amicable solution was reached, the Central Government would take steps to enforce the Supreme Court's opinion. To avoid ambiguity, the learned Solicitor General was asked to take instructions and put in writing the Central Government's position in this behalf: If the answer to the question posed by the Reference was that no Hindu temple or religious structure had stood on the disputed site prior to the construction of the disputed structure, would the disputed structure be rebuilt? On 14-9-1994, the learned Solicitor General made the following statement in response:

"Government stands by the policy of secularism and of even-handed treatment of all religious communities. The Acquisition of Certain Area at Ayodhya Act, 1993, as well as the Presidential Reference, have the objective of maintaining public order and promoting communal harmony and the spirit of common brotherhood amongst the people of India.

Government is committed to the construction of a Ram temple and a mosque, but their actual location will be determined only after the Supreme Court renders its opinion in the Presidential Reference.

Government will treat the finding of the Supreme Court on the question of fact referred under Article 143 of the Constitution as a verdict which is final and binding.

In the light of the Supreme Court's opinion and consistent with it, Government will make efforts to resolve the controversy by a process of negotiations. Government is confident that the opinion of the Supreme Court will have a salutary effect on the attitudes of the communities and they will no longer take conflicting positions on the factual issue settle by the Supreme Court.

If efforts at a negotiated settlement as aforesaid do not succeed, Government is committed to enforce a solution in the light of the Supreme Court's opinion and consistent with it, Government's action in this regard will be even-handed in respect of both the communities. If the question referred is answered in the affirmative, namely, that a Hindu temple/structure did exist prior to the construction of the demolished structure, Government action will be in support of the wishes of the Hindu community. If, on the other hand, the question is answered in the negative, namely, that no such Hindu temple/structure existed at the relevant time, then Government action will be in support of the wishes of the Muslim community.

106. The learned Solicitor General was asked to clarify whether the Central Government proposed to act in support of either community's wishes as presently known or as ascertained after the answer to the Reference was given and negotiations had failed. The learned Solicitor General was unable to get instructions in this behalf from the Central Government. It is fair to say that he had not much time to do so as the arguments were closed on the day after the clarification was sought.

107. It is relevant now to refer to the content of the dispute.

"At the centre of the dispute is the demand voiced by the Vishwa Hindu Parishad (VHP) and its allied organisations for the restoration of a site said to be the birthplace of Shri Ram in Ayodhya. Till 6-12-1992, this site was occupied by the structure erected in 1528 by Mir Baqi who claimed to have built it on orders of the first Mughal Emperor Babar.

* * *

The VHP and its allied organisations based their demand on the assertion that this site is the birthplace of Shri Ram and a Hindu temple commemorating this site stood here till it was destroyed on Babar's command and a masjid was erected in its place.

* * *

During the negotiations aimed at finding an amicable solution to the dispute one issue which came to the fore was whether a Hindu temple had existed on the site occupied by the disputed structure and whether it was demolished on Babar's order for the construction of the masjid .... It was stated by certain Muslim leaders that if these assertions were proved, the Muslims would voluntarily hand over the disputed shrine to the Hindus." (Paras 2.1, 2.2 and 2.3 of the White Paper.)

108. The Statement of Objects and Reasons for the Act states:

"It was considered necessary to acquire the site of the disputed structure and suitable adjacent land for setting up a complex....

Annexure A-4

The Destruction of Mecca

[October 1, 2014 p A-27]

When Malcolm X visited Mecca in 1964, he was enchanted. He found the city "as ancient as time itself," and wrote that the partly constructed extension to the Sacred Mosque "will surpass the architectural beauty of India's Taj Mahal."

Fifty years on, no one could possibly describe Mecca as ancient, or associate beauty with Islam's holiest city. Pilgrims performing the hajj this week will search in vain for Mecca's history.

The dominant architectural site in the city is not the Sacred Mosque, where the Kaaba, the symbolic focus of Muslims everywhere, is. It is the obnoxious Makkah Royal Clock Tower hotel, which, at 1,972 feet, is among the world's tallest buildings. It is part of a mammoth development of skyscrapers that includes luxury shopping malls and hotels catering to the superrich. The skyline is no longer dominated by the rugged outline of encircling peaks. Ancient mountains have been flattened. The city is now surrounded by the brutalism of rectangular steel and concrete structures—an amalgam of Disneyland and Las Vegas.

The "guardians" of the Holy City, the rulers of Saudi Arabia and the clerics, have a deep hatred of history. They want everything to look brand-new. Meanwhile, the sites are expanding to accommodate the rising number of pilgrims, up to almost three million today from 200,000 in the 1960s.

The initial phase of Mecca's destruction began in the mid-1970s, and I was there to witness it. Innumerable ancient buildings, including the Bilal mosque, dating from the time of the Prophet

Muhammad, were bulldozed. The old Ottoman houses, with their elegant mashrabiyas—latticework windows—and elaborately carved doors, were replaced with hideous modern ones. Within a few years, Mecca was transformed into a "modern" city with large multilane roads, spaghetti junctions, gaudy hotels and shopping malls.

The few remaining buildings and sites of religious and cultural significance were erased more recently. The Makkah Royal Clock Tower, completed in 2012, was built on the graves of an estimated 400 sites of cultural and historical significance, including the city's few remaining millennium-old buildings. Bulldozers arrived in the middle of the night, displacing families that had lived there for centuries. The complex stands on top of Ajyad Fortress, built around 1780, to protect Mecca from bandits and invaders. The house of Khadijah, the first wife of the Prophet Muhammad, has been turned into a block of toilets. The Makkah Hilton is built over the house of Abu Bakr, the closest companion of the prophet and the first caliph.

Apart from the Kaaba itself, only the inner core of the Sacred Mosque retains a fragment of history. It consists of intricately carved marble columns, adorned with calligraphy of the names of the prophet's companions. Built by a succession of Ottoman sultans, the columns date from the early 16th century. And yet plans are afoot to demolish them, along with the whole of the interior of the Sacred Mosque, and to replace it with an ultramodern doughnut-shaped building.

The only other building of religious significance in the city is the house where the Prophet Muhammad lived. During most of the Saudi era it was used first as a cattle market, then turned into a library, which is not open to the people. But even this is too much for the radical Saudi clerics who have repeatedly called for its demolition. The clerics fear that, once inside, pilgrims would pray to the prophet, rather than to God—an unpardonable sin. It is only a matter of time before it is razed and turned, probably, into a parking lot.

The cultural devastation of Mecca has radically transformed the city. Unlike Baghdad, Damascus and Cairo, Mecca was never a great intellectual and cultural center of Islam. But it was always a pluralistic city where debate among different Muslim sects and schools of thought was not unusual. Now it has been reduced to a monolithic religious entity where only one, ahistoric, literal interpretation of Islam is permitted, and where all other sects, outside of the Salafist brand of Saudi Islam, are regarded as false. Indeed, zealots frequently threaten pilgrims of different sects. Last year, a group of Shiite pilgrims from Michigan were attacked with knives by extremists, and in August, a coalition of American Muslim groups wrote to the State Department asking for protection during this year's hajj.

The erasure of Meccan history has had a tremendous impact on the hajj itself. The word "hajj" means effort. It is through the effort of traveling to Mecca, walking from one ritual site to another, finding and engaging with people from different cultures and sects, and soaking in the history of Islam that the pilgrims acquired knowledge as well as spiritual fulfillment. Today, hajj is a packaged tour, where you move, tied to your group, from hotel to hotel, and seldom encounter people of different cultures and ethnicities. Drained of history and religions and cultural plurality, hajj is no longer a transforming, once-in-a-lifetime spiritual experience. It has been reduced to a mundane exercise in rituals and shopping.

Mecca is a microcosm of the Muslim world. What happens to and in the city has a profound effect on Muslims everywhere. The spiritual heart of Islam is an ultramodern, monolithic enclave, where difference is not tolerated, history has no meaning, and consumerism is paramount. It is hardly surprising then that literalism, and the murderous interpretations of Islam associated with it, have become so dominant in Muslim lands.

Ziauddin Sardar is the editor of the quarterly Critical Muslim and the author of "Mecca: The Sacred City."

A version of this op-ed appears in print on October 1, 2014, on page A27 of the New York edition with the headline: The Destruction of Mecca.

Annexure A-5

Islam Question and Answer

152263: Should the mosque be sold or demolished when the inhabitants leave?

We have a mosque in our location where we say our regular prayer including JUMMA prayer. Now we are leaving the complex and this complex is going to be handed over to another people who are non-muslims. Basically it is their complex. We have been here for our temporary duty for six years. Now after completion of our duty we leaving it to them. So. what to do with the mosque? Should we break it down or keep it as it? As they are non-muslims, none is going to say prayer there unless Allah wishes otherwise. Again if we leave it as it is there is scope of misuse. Please advise us what to do with the mosque?

Praise be to Allaah.

If the waqf is no longer of benefit and it is not possible to benefit from it, it is permissible to sell it according to the correct scholarly opinion, whether it is a mosque or anything else. If the people of the mosque are moving to another place and there will no longer be any one who could benefit from it, it is permissible to sell it and use the money to build another mosque.

Ibn Qudaamah may Allah have mercy on him said: If a waqf falls into disrepair and is no longer of any benefit, such as if a house collapses and it is not possible to rebuild it, or the people of the village move away from a mosque so people no longer pray in the mosque, or it has become too small for the congregation and it is not possible to expand it where it is, or if its walls have developed cracks and it is not possible to repair them or part of them except by selling part of it, then it is permissible to sell part of it in order to repair the rest of it.

If it is not possible to benefit from any part of it, it is permissible to sell the whole of it.

Imam Ahmad said: If there are two wooden beams in the mosque that are of value, it is permissible to sell them and spend the money on the mosque.

He also said: A mosque may be moved if there is the fear of thieves, if its location is dirty? Al-Qaadi said: i.e., if that is keeping people from praying in it.

End quote from al-Mughni, 5/368.

Shaykh Ibn Baaz (may Allah have mercy on him) said:

If the waqf is no longer of benefit, whether it is a mosque or otherwise, it is permissible to sell it according to the more correct of the two scholarly opinions, and its price may be spent on another waqf of equal value to replace the first waqf if possible. It was narrated from Ameer al-Mu'mineen 'Umar ibn al-Khattaab (may Allah be pleased with him) that he issued instructions that the mosque of Kufah be moved to another location because there was an interest that could be served by doing so. Therefore when a mosque is no longer of any benefit at all, it is more appropriate to suggest that it is permissible to move it. However, this is a matter concerning which there is a difference of opinion among the scholars, but the reliable view is that it is permissible because Islamic sharee'ah is perfect and came to achieve and fulfill what is in people's best interests and to cancel and reduce that which is detrimental to their interests; it enjoins preserving wealth and forbids neglecting or wasting it. There is no doubt that if a waqf is no longer effective there is no interest to be served by keeping it; rather keeping it is a waste of money. So it should be sold and the money spent on something similar.

End quote from Fataawa ash-Shaykh Ibn Baaz, 20/11

If this mosque can be sold to someone who will use it for something permissible, such as a hospital for example, after removing its minaret and changing its appearance, it is permissible to sell it as it is, without demolishing it, because of the interest that will be served which is to bring a higher price than if (the land) were to be sold after demolishing it.

If there is the fear that it will be used for some haraam purpose, then it is to be demolished and the land sold, and the money should be spent on another mosque.

And Allah knows best.

Annexure A-6

Demolishing a Mosque for Public Works

Q. *Is it allowed in Islam for the government to destroy a mosque in order to build something else like public roads and rebuild the mosque somewhere else?*

Answered by Sheikh Muhammad Muhammad Salim Abd al-Wadud.

The mosque is an endowment (waqf) and is subject to the rulings of an endowment.

Endowment properties can be relocated whenever the overwhelming interests of society are concerned, or in order to prevent harm to the public. This is under the state's jurisdiction to decide in consideration of necessity (darurah) and need (hajah). In countries where the state is not involved, the relevant Muslim authorities in charge of the specific trust will be the ones to make the decision.

The Companions moved the graves of the martyrs of Uhud—exhuming and reburying their bodies—in order to facilitate the waterworks of the city of Madinah. It is well-known in Islamic Law that a grave remains an endowment connected with the deceased until the body of the deceased is fully decomposed. Nevertheless, the Companions moved those graves due to considerations of public welfare.

Therefore, if the authorities determine that there is a valid need to demolish a mosque building and relocate the mosque to some other suitable locality, then it falls within the state's jurisdiction to do so. This could be in order to facilitate essential public works or in order to secure the welfare of the mosque community, by providing them with a larger or more conveniently located mosque. In either case, the state must bear the full expense of relocating the mosque.

And Allah knows best.